MELLEN STUDIES
IN LITERATURE/JACOBEAN DRAMA

JOHN WEBSTER:
Politics and Tragedy

Robert P. Griffin

The Edwin Mellen Press
Lewiston•Queenston•Lampeter

ISBN 0-7734-0458-9

The Edwin Mellen Press
Box 450
Lewiston, `New York
USA 14092-0450

The Edwin Mellen Press
Box 67
Queenston, Ontario
CANADA L0S 1L0

The Edwin Mellen Press, Ltd.
Lampeter, Ceredigion, Wales
UNITED KINGDOM SA48 8LT

Printed in the United States of America

CONTENTS

INTRODUCTION   1

CHAPTER I JACOBEAN POLITICS   4

Notes to Chapter I   36

CHAPTER II THE WHITE DEVIL   50

Notes to Chapter II   92

CHAPTER III THE DUCHESS OF MALFI   105

Notes to Chapter III   134

CHAPTER IV APPIUS AND VIRGINIA   140

Notes to Chapter IV   168

BIBLIOGRAPHY   175

Introduction

Tragedy is a literary form in which the playwright
discovers and gives shape to basic conflicts within the culture of his own time. For John Webster and certain of his
contemporaries the conflict was the obsessive Renaissance
one between an ideal of order and anarchic will. Unlike
their Elizabethan predecessors, however, for the Jacobeans
the issue was essentially political, and in a way peculiar
to their generation. The link between politics and
morality, which has since become attenuated, was all important,
suggesting a view of man perhaps closer to the pagan-political
than the medieval-religious. With Webster as with Aristotle,
political things were first things.

After the death of Elizabeth and the accession of
James I, there occurred in England a crisis of political
authority occasioned by the collapse of the Tudor myth of
divine right. Lacking the legitimacy provided by a belief
in divine ordination, the royal court could no longer provide
the informing idealism required to maintain what Max Weber
called the necessary "reigning fictions" every governing body
needs to rule. The generation of playwrights most affected
by this crisis was Webster's own, and we must understand
this fact to appreciate the fascination exerted upon its
imagination by tales of Italian Renaissance murder and

intrigue, and by the political thought of Machiavelli. The collapse of the divine right theory left a vacuum into which flowed the myth of the Machiavellian politician, appearing temporarily to represent the whole truth about men and power, and imaged in the world of the Italian Renaissance court on the Jacobean stage.

By the close of the second decade of the century, however, the crisis had passed. Theories of Stoicism and natural right came again to dominate political consciousness, placing Machiavelli's thought in perspective. A new vision of political possibility asserted itself, and with the passing of the generation, the crisis itself passed.

Webster's three tragedies reflect this crisis and its passing. The tragic sense of inevitability in The White Devil (1612) and The Duchess of Malfi (1614) emerges from Webster's depiction, in moralistic terms, the choices offered by the Machiavellian view of political reality: to flee from participation in public life and thereby forego one's claim to personal glory; or to seek honor at court, participating thereby in obvious corruption and immorality. The two plays together examine this range of political possibility without discovering a solution. Both plays depict the same world but each from a slightly different perspective. And though neither discovers a way out, the second play does penetrate through the Machiavellian myth to show the insufficiency of its claims to the complete truth. Webster's last tragedy,

Appius and Virginia (1625-27), is more secular auto than
tragedy, celebrating as it does the pieties of post-Jacobean
politics. Whatever his personal involvement may have been,
the playwright's vision of political reality in this last
play has none of the tragic inevitability of the earlier
plays. Thus Webster's career would seem to encompass both
the peak and the passing of Jacobean political tragedy.

CHAPTER I

JACOBEAN POLITICS

For a brief period in the first quarter of the
seventeenth century in England the political thought of
Machiavelli came to dominate the consciousness of a large
number of people. The collapse of the divine right myth
left a vacuum into which the idea of the Machiavellian
politician, imaged in the world of Machiavellian Italy on
the Jacobean stage,[1] flowed, appearing temporarily to
represent the whole truth about men and power.

Describing every culture as a dialectic, Lionel
Trilling has observed that there are artists

> who contain a large part of the dialectic within them-
> selves, their meaning and their power lying in their
> contradictions; they contain within themselves, it
> may be said, the very essence of the culture. . . .[2]

John Webster was one of these, as both his strengths and
weaknesses attest. The poetry of his tragedy comes out
of his having tapped, briefly, the central problem of his
age, the problem of "anarchic will."[3]

To understand this dialectic and its expression in
Webster's art, it will be necessary first to say something
about the background of Jacobean politics, and then to show
how this was metamorphosed into tragedy; thus what follows

in Chapter I is both historical background and critical theory.

1

> Not all the water in the rough rude sea
> Can wash the balm from an anointed king;
> The breath of worldly men cannot depose
> The deputy elected by the Lord.
>   --Shakespeare, <u>Richard II</u>

Between the first years of the seventeenth century and 1649 the English attitude toward the monarchy underwent an immense change.

In January 1649 an English King was brought to trial on a charge of abusing the trust placed in him by his subjects, was convicted, and was publicly and ceremoniously beheaded, after which the Monarchy was abolished and a Republic proclaimed. Nothing like it had ever happened in European history before. For a thousand years Englishmen had been in the habit of murdering tiresome or inconvenient kings . . . but never before had an anointed king been formally brought to book.[4]

The imaginative power of the idea of kingship under the Tudors has been treated at considerable length,[5] and accounts of the history of the first half of the seventeenth

century are surprisingly complete and detailed. What is
not so well understood, however, is the process by which
a concept such as divine right is radically altered, and
furthermore, how this affects an artist's vision of the
real and the possible.

As a point of departure, I would suggest we might
look to Shakespeare's use of the divine right myth in
Macbeth, attempting thereby a working definition of the
concept itself.

In Macbeth to kill a king means a good deal more
than the violation of human law; it means the disruption
of Nature itself. And it is precisely this which suggests
analogy with Greek tragedy. Like Greek tragedy, Macbeth
is theological: both involve belief in some immortal prin-
ciple operative in the universe, called Nature or God,
and containing within itself a gyroscopic mechanism which
operates to restore equilibrium whenever it is temporarily
upset by the actions of mortal men. Though Macbeth's crimes
strike heaven on the face, with the turn of the seasons
all is made whole again.[6]

To understand the concept of divine right as it
appears with all its popular theological and poetic rami-
fications in a play like Macbeth requires an historical
approach, since political theories usually only acquire
their religious overlay with the passage of time. Its
particular manifestation in the Tudor myth that was so
useful to Shakespeare may thus be seen as a segment, in

England quite nearly the final one, of a larger continuum.

The theory (or doctrine) of the divine right of kings was a direct outgrowth of the conflict of church and state. As is the case with every theory of power, the divine right theory had as its raison d'etre its practical assistance to power.[7] When the various national princes broke with the Roman church they converted the right of sovereignty, a right which until then had been accorded only as a limited mandate, into a free-hold. Previously something of a liability, since the prince held authority only through the church, the divine right concept was to become his chief asset.[8] St. Paul's "There is no power but of God: the powers that be are ordained by God," had provided over the centuries a theological explanation of power which was fully comprehensive, including as it did every instance of power.[9] It continued to do so under the myth of the divine right of kings.

When we recall the exalted and sacred place enjoyed by the monarchy as a result of its evolution under the Tudors, it becomes less difficult to understand the dynamics of power in the early decades of the seventeenth century. Thus the situation must be viewed from the historical, for power can be understood only as a stage in its own evolution.

All societies, even those which seem to us the least developed, go back into a past of several

thousand years, and the authorities which ruled them
in former times did not disappear without bequeathing
to their successors their prestige, nor without leaving
in men's minds imprints which are cumulative in their
effect. The succession of governments which, in the
course of centuries, rule the same society may be
looked on as one underlying government which takes
on continuous accretions. And for that reason Power
is something which the historian, rather than the
logician, comprehends.[10]

During the final years of the sixteenth century,
especially after 1588, the English royal court served more
than ever as a focus of national sentiment. But it was the
person of the monarch which provided the cynosure, the symbol
by means of which the aggregate became a whole. The twentieth
century political philosopher, Bertrand de Jouvenal, sees
such a stage as inevitable in the evolution of every
nation-state:

> . . . it is on the throne that the nation is based.
> Men become compatriots by reason of their allegiance
> to one and the same person. And now we see why it
> is that peoples formed in the monarchical mould
> inevitably regard the nation as a person; they think
> by analogy from the living person through whom a
> common sentiment has been formed.[11]

Thus the monarch can be seen as functioning as a suppositious being living outside and above the people, an Archimedian point so to speak, serving to combine religious ideology and national aspiration in a single center. With this fact in mind we may begin to comprehend the absolute necessity for the maintenance of appearances on the part of the monarch.

2

                    Come, let's away
    to prison:
We two alone will sing like birds i' the cage:
When thou dost ask me blessing, I'll kneel down,
And ask of thee forgiveness: so we'll live,
And pray, and sing, and tell old tales, and laugh,
At gilded butterflies, and hear poor rogues
Talk of court news; and we'll talk with them too,
Who loses and who wins; who's in, who's out;
And take upon's the mystery of things,
As if we were God's spies; and we'll wear out,
In a wall'd prison, packs and sects of great ones,
That ebb and flow by the moon.
                    --Shakespeare, King Lear

    After Elizabeth's death and the accession of King James political reality changed radically; and equally

important, because James possessed none of Elizabeth's
political skill, this change became visible to all who
would see. A new image of the royal court began to emerge.
While it is perhaps impossible to demonstrate the change
in mood Professor Ellis-Fermor contends accompanied this
political change, it is possible to show the change itself
and to explore some of the implications for the drama of
the period.[12] Implicit in Professor Ellis-Fermor's view
is the historically demonstrable fact of a shift from a
private and personal concept of monarchy to a public and
comparatively impersonal one which took place in the popular consciousness within a relatively brief span of
years.[13] Thus it is that the change in the popular image
of the monarchy may be viewed as both cause and effect:
impersonal forces over which James could have had little
if any control linked up with those of a personal kind,[14]
and the consequence was a political crisis of authority,[15]
one which served to make accessible to poets and playwrights
a conflict of individual will and authority that is always
potential in the human situation.

  With this failure of authority, the monarchy which
once had served to embody all that was sacred comes to be
blamed for all that is corrupt and evil. And in the case
of a monarch ignorant or careless of appearances such as
King James, a public scandal is inevitable. In the words
of one of his contemporary critics:

> Nor was his love [for successive favorites] carried
> on with a discretion sufficient to cover a less scan-
> dalous behavior, for the kings kissing them after so
> lascivious a mode in publick, and upon the theatre,
> as it were, of the world, prompted many to imagine
> some things done in the tyring-house, that exceed my
> expression no lesse than they do my experience: and
> therefore left floating upon the waves of conjecture,
> which hath in my hearing tossed them from one side to
> another.[16]

The shock waves were most severe close to the center, especially among those belonging to the aristocracy
created by the Tudor dynasty.[17] Used to looking to the
monarch and to the court to provide a coherent sense for
life, since under a monarchy it is the personal glory available within the public space provided by the court that
is the motivating force for the whole body politic, they
were left under James I with the equally devastating choices
of participating in what was obviously corrupt in an effort
to gain whatever precarious immortality might be achievable
from an attenuated and dying center of power, or leaving
the court for the obscurity of private life.[18]

The immediate consequence of the passing of the
historical mystique I have been discussing was a temporary
period of crisis, during which, as we shall see, Machiavelli's
theory came into its own. By the early 1620's, however,

natural right theory, "which in some sense ruled speculation from Cicero to Rousseau,"[19] again made itself felt in
the realm of practical political affairs. According to
Cassirer,

> the influence of Stoic thought [the source of natural
> right theory] had been unbroken and continuous. We
> can trace it to Roman jurisprudence, in the Fathers
> of the Church, in scholastic philosophy. But all this
> then had a theoretical interest rather than an imme-
> diate practical effect. The tremendous practical sig-
> nificance of this great stream of thought did not
> appear until the seventeenth and eighteenth centuries.
> Henceforward the theory of the natural rights of man
> was no longer an abstract ethical doctrine but one of
> the mainsprings of political action.[20]

Looked at from the perspective of a temporary break
in the traditional way of viewing man and his place in
society, the generation[21] of playwrights for whom the
Machiavel was particularly significant may be seen to share
a unique vision; or at least the potential for such a vision,
since for many it produced only sound and fury. Before
discussing the forms of these tragedies, however, it is
necessary to examine the Renaissance world of realpolitic
which they reflected.

3

> To lose one's life is a little thing. . . .
> But to see the sense of this life dissipated,
> to see our reason for existence disappear;
> that is what is insupportable.
>
>   --Camus, _Caligula_

It is important to note that the triumph of Machiavelli's thought in England had to wait upon the appropriate
historical circumstances, not the least of which was the
beginning of the decline of the monarchy. Since this shift
in the center of power has been thoroughly documented, there
is no need to discuss it here; it suffices to note that this
eclipse coincides historically with the scientific revolution in thought which served to undermine the entire
Renaissance system of values, religious and secular.[22]

In the realm of the political it was the analytic
mode of Machiavelli which stood ready at hand to replace,
maxim for maxim, the older system of values. And thus it
was that Machiavelli's thought severed the connection between statecraft and the practice of private virtue. For
the Machiavellian statesman the good of the state is the
only moral imperative. Tracing the rise of the secular
state to Machiavelli, Ernst Cassirer describes the consequence of the acceptance of his doctrine thus:

With Machiavelli we stand at the gateway of the modern

world. The desired end is attained; the state has
won its full autonomy. Yet this result has had to be
bought dearly. The state is entirely independent;
but at the same time it is completely isolated.
The sharp knife of Machiavelli's thought has cut off
all the threads by which in former generations the
state was fastened to the organic whole of human existence. The political world has lost its connection
not only with religion or metaphysics but also with
all the other forms of man's ethical and cultural
life. It stands alone--in an empty space.[23]

By casting his thought in the traditional form
of the handbook for princes, Machiavelli made it difficult
for Renaissance statesmen to ignore him. The fact that the
only teacher of princes Machiavelli mentions is Chiron,
the centaur who taught Achilles and many other ancient
princes, would make little difference, since the pattern
for the medieval and Renaissance instruction book was
classical. Respecting the Bible, his method is simply to
ignore the whole idea of revealed truth. His own model
is a mythical figure, half beast and half man; thus he
returns in both form and theme to the foundation of human
society. He urges princes to make use of both natures,
the human and the beast; but he builds his argument by
repeating the essential: a prince must imitate the beast--
that is, use the person of the fox and the lion, or imitate

those two natures. The imitation of the beast takes the
place of the imitation of God.

Machiavelli was correct in seeing the beast-man
as an imaginative creation of the ancient writers; but to
conclude, as he seems to have done, that they meant by
such a figure that man may transcend himself only in the
direction of the sub-human was incorrect. Machiavelli's
beast-man is, however, scientific rather than mythic, and
the scientific naturalism which governs Machiavelli's thought
makes his employment of myth radically different from that
of the ancient writers.[24]

By way of illustrating how ancient myth served to
embody a particular truth, but not necessarily the whole
truth, about man and his environment, we might examine the
figure of the Minotaur, especially since it will serve also
to clarify something of what the ancients felt to be the
true nature of politics, a humanistic vision lost with the
triumph of Machiavellian realpolitic.

The Minotaur, as we recall, was born to Queen
Pasiphaë, wife to Minos, king of the island-empire of
Crete in the period of its commercial supremacy. The
bull which fathered the monster had been sent from the
sea by Poseidon long before as the sign which designated
Minos, of all the contenders, King of Crete. But Minos
had vowed to sacrifice the animal immediately, as an
offering and symbol of service. Minos, however, failed to

carry out his vow because of personal avarice, thus con-
verting a public event to personal gain. According to
Joseph Campbell's account,

> the whole sense of his investiture as king had been
> that he was no longer a mere private person. The re-
> turn of the bull should have symbolized his absolutely
> selfless submission to the functions of his role.
> The retaining of it represented, on the other hand,
> an impulse to egocentric self-aggrandizement.

Such an imaginative construct is of course endlessly
suggestive. Minos himself was, as we recall, the product of
a union between a beast-god and a human mother, suggesting
that the human condition is to undergo the self-same cycle
again and again. The fate of Crete was to give way before
the rising power of the mainland city-states, and thus we
may view the myth of the Minotaur as an expression of
Time's revenge, wherein the egoism of command leads to its
own destruction. To quote Campbell once more,

> The inflated ego of the tyrant is a curse to himself
> and his world--no matter how his affairs may seem to
> prosper. Self-terrorized, fear haunted, alert at
> every hand to meet and battle back the anticipated
> aggressions of his environment, which are primarily
> the reflections of the uncontrollable impulses to
> acquisition within himself, the giant of self-achieved

independence is the world's messenger of disaster,

even though, in the mind, he may entertain himself

with humane intentions.[25]

Machiavelli's naturalistic approach to man, which

has an exact scientific counterpart in Galileo's basic

assumption that matter is unalterable,[26] made him more

psychologist than philosopher, which helps to explain how,

despite his obvious insight into human motivation, he could

fail to understand the humanistic truth not only of the

Bible but of the classics which he so loved as well. His

new philosophy is supposedly based on how men live as

distinguished from how they ought to live; it despises the

utopian, and it understands man in the light of the sub-

human rather than the super-human.[27] In the realm of the

political, according to Leo Strauss,

> The consequence is an enormous simplification and,
>
> above all, the appearance of the discovery of a
>
> hitherto wholly unsuspected whole continent. In
>
> fact, however, Machiavelli does not bring to light
>
> a single political phenomenon of any fundamental
>
> importance which was not fully known to the classics.
>
> His seeming discovery is only the reverse side of
>
> the oblivion of the most important: all things
>
> necessarily appear in a new light if they are seen
>
> for the first time in a specifically dimmed light.
>
> A stupendous contraction of the horizon appears to

Machiavelli and his successors as a wondrous enlarge-
ment of the horizon.[28]

Although his views seem familiar enough to the
modern reader,[29] they were strong medicine to the Jacobean
"new men," especially those who wanted confirmation of the
"legitimacy" of their own aspirations.[30] The very newness
of Machiavelli's ideas had its attraction, and the carefully
pragmatic Bacon nodded approvingly.[31] If further confirmation
that Machiavelli was correct about men and power were needed,
there was the spectacle of Renaissance Italy; had not
Machiavelli formulated his theories on the basis of his
observations of political actuality in his homeland?[32]
Theodore Spencer suggests we may understand the subversive
menace of Machiavelli's ideas to Renaissance moralists
by comparing The Prince and the Discourses on Livy with
the De Officiis of Cicero:

> For the De Officiis represents the official sixteenth-
> century doctrine concerning the behavior of man as
> a governor. It was universally read; apart from many
> editions in Latin, there were at least eleven editions
> of the work in English between 1534 and 1616, and no
> sixteenth-century treatise on government was without
> some indebtedness to it.
> According to Cicero, if man is to control his
> fellow men and himself, justice is the essential
> virtue, and moral right is the basis of action.[33]

My conviction is, however, that no amount of philosophical speculation will have much effect in the political
realm without the stimulus of actual events, and as I have
attempted to show, these events--the failure of the court
to maintain appearances, the shift of power away from the
monarch, and the rise of the new men of power--were real
and conspicuous. And it was this current image of political reality during the early years of the seventeenth century
that gave substance to the heretofore merely speculative and
theoretical.

When one considers the fact that Machiavelli's type
of statecraft had been widely current in practice since the
dawn of human society one must disagree with the description,
advanced most recently by Herbert Butterfield, of Machiavelli
as a doctrinaire who wrote an operational code.[34] Putting
aside considerations of what is truly admirable in Machia-
velli--the fearlessness of his thought, the scope of his
vision, and the grace of his style--one must agree, I believe,
with the conclusion that it was what he offered to the actual
or would-be rulers that accounts for his impact upon the age;
through him, according to the political theorist James
Meisel,

The new men are given a clean bill of health, they
are presented with the gift of a good conscience.
By imparting to them their stern duties, Machiavelli
is, by implication, stating their new rights as well.

By brushing aside the objections of the old morality,
he clears the ground on which the modern state,
conceived in illegality, could grow to be legitimate.
The Prince was to encourage the spread of an intellectual climate which would make that new legality ac-
ceptable.[35]

Finally, the fact that we are able to see the flaws
in Machiavelli's reasoning is no real argument that the
seventeenth-century Englishman would have been able to
also. What characterizes the historical myth, and just as
divine right was a species of historical myth so too was
the Machiavellian myth, is not that it is necessarily false,
but that its truth cannot be established from historical
evidence. As Cassirer writes, "The problem is not the
material content of mythology but the intensity with which
it is experienced, with which it is believed--as only something endowed with objective reality it can be believed."[36]

Professor Jerome Bruner, psychologist and cultural
historian, attempts to pull together many of the same issues
I have been dealing with here. Commenting on the necessity
of myth to men's sense of identity, he goes on to discuss
the various and (in Western culture from the time of the
Greeks) changing idealizations of the man of superior knowledge and competence, then attempts to delineate the process
by which he becomes objectified in literature. Most of this
is not new of course.[37] But Bruner concludes with an

interesting insight into what may happen when a society is temporarily bereft of one of its dominant myths, is no longer what Joseph Campbell would call the "mythologically instructed community."[38] He describes the process by which new myths of identity are tried out, so to speak, and how those which prove to be unsatisfactory are discarded and replaced by others. The trying out has traditionally been the job of work of the artist, the poet especially, and it is this which has immemorially given him his preternatural place in the community.

As Frye would have it, the job of work of the poet is "to humanize" the natural world, "to make a home of an environment."[39] Even sophisticated cultures, such as was late Renaissance England, may find themselves temporarily plunged into what appears to be a hostile "state of nature," where even the most traditional and time-honored roles and conventions become threatening and unreal.[40] In such an emotional-intellectual context, the London stage, traditionally a focus of national consciousness, could not but reflect and modify the popular image of political man.

4

. . . I think the king is but a man, as I am. The violet smells to him as it doth to me; the element shows to him as it doth to me; all his senses have but human conditions.

His ceremonies laid by, in his naked-

ness he appears but a man. . . .

--Shakespeare, Henry V

If dramatic literature is in part a response to
its culture, it is also, and probably more importantly
over the long view, in part conditioned by its literary
context and the tradition. Moreover, these influences
interact in a way difficult if not impossible to separate.[41]
In the immediately following, I shall treat this interaction
in summary fashion by focusing on Shakespeare and then on
the literary convention of the stage Machiavel, with the
intention of making this introductory material on politics
and the age, and its connection with the drama, less
theoretical and speculative.

The idea of divine right had in England, as we have
seen, the historical function of what we should call a myth,

a large, controlling image that gives philosophical

meaning to the facts of ordinary life; that is, which

has   organizing value of experience. . . . Without

such images, experience is chaotic, fragmentary and

merely phenomenal. . . . All real convictions involve

a mythology, either in its usual, broad sense or in

a private sense. In the first case it is embodied in

literature or in ritual or in both, in which it has

application to the whole of a society and tends to
be religious. In the second, it remains in the realm
of fantasy, in which it tends to be obsessive and
fanatical. This is not to say that sound myths of general application necessarily support religions; rather
that they perform the historical functions of religion--
they unify experience in a way that is satisfactory
to the whole culture and to the whole personality.[42]

While the center holds, the dramatic genre characteristic
of this stage in a nation's history is, according to Northrop
Frye, the secular auto, which he describes as

a romantic drama presenting the exploits of a hero,
which is closely related to tragedy, the end of a
hero's exploit being eventually his death, but which
in itself is neither tragic nor comic, being primarily
spectacular.

He cites Marlowe's Tamburlaine as an illustration of the
type but notes that the English Renaissance audience was
"too bourgeois for a chivalric drama to get firmly established, and the Elizabethan secular auto eventually became
the history play."[43]

Renaissance theories of art also favored such a
focus. Most literary critical theory of the age had a
social rather than aesthetic basis: the difference between
the various types of drama was made to depend upon subject

matter, and this in turn, to depend upon the social class
of the characters of the tale.[44] English Renaissance theory
of tragedy was borrowed almost entirely from sixteenth-
century Italian criticism, which derived ultimately from
classical sources, though many of the aesthetically important aspects of Aristotle and other classical theorists became
lost in the process. To Renaissance England tragedy still
meant what it had to Chaucer and the Middle Ages generally,
the fall of a man from high place. Chaucer's Monk in the
Canterbury Tales begins his collection of tragic tales with,

> I wol biwaille, in manere of tragedie,
> The harm of hem that stoode in heigh degree.

The didactic intent carried over also, remaining
at least superficially important through the period of
Shakespeare's last and greatest plays. Sir Philip Sidney
in his Defence of Poesie is quite explicit about the moral
function of tragedy:

> Tragedy . . . openeth the greatest wounds, and shew-
> eth forth the Ulcers that are covered with Tissue;
> that maketh Kinges feare to be Tyrants, and the
> Tyrants manifest their tirannicall humors.[45]

A critical commonplace of Renaissance critics and
artists was that the function of art is to reflect nature,
the real world of men, their institutions and concerns.

Such a theory represents the mainstream of Western critical theory all the way from Aristotle to the English Romantic
revolt of the late eighteenth century. A recently pub-
lished history of criticism traces this mainstream, emphasizing in particular the role of descriptive metaphor, especially
the art-as-mirror figure, in controlling and limiting both
theory and practice.[46] It suffices to note here that, by and
large, Renaissance critics gave complete allegiance to this
conception of art.

Contemporary scholars and critics of Elizabethan
and seventeenth century literature have come more and more
to recognize the importance of the link between the art of
the time and an artist's vision of the world, and especially
his critical preconceptions. Francis Fergusson writes, "the
Elizabethan theater was itself a mirror which had been formed
at the center of the culture of its time, and at the center
of the life and awareness of the community."[47] The use by
Shakespeare and his fellow dramatists of the Tudor myth made
the image of the court central to the theater of the age. In
an essay on Shakespeare's Richard II, Professor Dean traces
the state-theater image which dominates that play to two
sources, Christian Humanism and Renaissance realpolitic,
drawing his representative illustrations from the works of
Thomas More and Machiavelli.[48] One might argue, I believe,
that the problem of anarchic will I have noted in connection
with Webster is central also to Shakespeare's tragedy, and

that it was present all through the history plays, becoming
explicit only later in the tragedies themselves. In Webster
the issue is political from the first, in large part because
he wrote his tragedies during the brief period when Jacobean
London saw its most important questions objectified in
political terms.

There would seem to me, therefore, to be a distinct
difference between the image of political reality in
Shakespeare's histories and in the political plays of Webster
and several of his contemporaries. According to John Palmer,
Shakespeare contemplated the political as such in a mood of
"ironic detachment."

> He was impartial because he was in the last resort
> indifferent. . . . He was interested in persons and
> many of them just happened to have been public per-
> sons.[49]

And E. M. W. Tillyard on the history plays notes that the
order against which Shakespeare judges his characters was
"much more than political order, or, if political, was
always a part of a larger cosmic order."[50] Shakespeare's
universe necessarily included the political, for, to quote
Palmer again, "Elizabethans expected to find upon the
stage kings, princes, and generals." And on Shakespeare's
insight into public character he writes:

> The astonishing veracity of Shakespeare's political

characters is due, indeed, to the small interest which
he took in politics as compared with the great interest which he took in human nature. His main concern
was not so much with the politics as with the men who
made them. He was immune from political bias and his
political characters are therefore true for all time.[51]

There is a sharp contrast between the attitude
described above and that of Webster, who seems to have
contemplated the political with the intensity of one of his
own heroes:

. . . Princes images on their tombs

Do not lie, as they were wont, seeming to pray

Up to heaven: but with their hands under their cheekes,

(As if they died of the tooth-ache)--they are not carved

With their eies fix'd upon the starres; but as

Their minds were wholy bent upon the world,

The selfe-same way they seeme to turne their faces.

(The Duchess of Malfi, IV, ii, 153-59)[52]

Political reality in Shakespeare, despite the awareness of realpolitic, is still medieval. Tillyard is right
in seeing Shakespeare's vision of the political as part of
"a larger cosmic order," although he appears to attribute
this in the above quotation to a primary, even exclusive,
interest in character. What seems clear enough is the
fact that there is something essentially Elizabethan rather

than Jacobean about Shakespeare's history plays, and perhaps
even the tragedies, with the possible exception of Lear.
The problem plays, however, seem perfectly at home in a
Jacobean context, and this is a consequence of the political
focus in such plays as Troilus and Cressida and, especially,
Measure for Measure. Interestingly enough, Francis Fergusson
has suggested the basic situation in Measure for Measure, the
disappearance of the Duke, was Shakespeare's device "to show
London the properties of government in the experimental
situation of Vienna.

> . . . When the Duke departs and leaves Angelo in charge,
> he sets the city a practical problem in government.
> The city unfolds the properties of government by try-
> ing all the wrong moves; and the Duke is at hand to
> reinforce the painful lessons in his counsel to Isa-
> bella or to Claudio, and at last by the order which,
> as temporal ruler, he can impose. . . .[53]

And perhaps this is as close as Shakespeare was to come to
apprehending the conflict which seems to me central to
Webster's tragedy: the loss of a moral exemplar in the person of a divinely ordained figure of political authority.

5

It is also possible to differentiate the Elizabethan
and the Jacobean in Renaissance tragedy in terms of a

particular literary convention such as the stage Machiavel.
In the following paragraphs I will be leaning heavily on
Robert Ornstein's recent account, partly because he is so comprehensive and partly because I believe him to be mistaken
about the Machiavel figure in Webster.

In his first chapter, Ornstein offers a devastating
criticism of the theses of E. M. W. Tillyard and Theodore
Spencer.[54] Tillyard contended that the age of Shakespeare
was able to produce great tragedy because of the very
security of humanistic ideals; Spencer's contention was that
it was the collapse of the so-called Elizabethan world view,
its humanistic ideals and values subverted by Machiavelli,
Montaigne, and Copernicus, that brought about the ideological
and moral crisis which made tragedy possible.[55] Ornstein
argues that the subversion of this essentially medieval world
view had been going forward for centuries. "What we call
'the Elizabethan World Picture' died quietly of old age,
cherished by the metaphysical poets and by Milton long after
it had ceased to interest seventeenth-century philosophers,"
he writes.[56] His case is impressive indeed, and he would
seem to have formidable support in recent scholarship in
the history of philosophy and scientific thought.[57] Ornstein
warns against the easy tendency "to exaggerate the subversive
influence of ideas the Jacobeans themselves did not find
greatly disturbing," and concludes that the crisis in values
which the tragedy of the age reflects is epistemological
rather than moral.

As I understand him, he is suggesting (1) that
although Jacobean tragic thought shared certain elements
with the thought of its day, to be understood it must be
viewed in terms of its own evolution, within the context
of its own period, roughly from Chapman to Ford; and (2)
that the climate of uncertainty which engendered the
tragedians' peculiar portraits of vice and depravity was
largely caused, not by the challenge of anti-humanistic
thought, but by the epistemological revolution which transformed the humanistic and created the scientific approach
to man and nature in the late Renaissance. The dramatists
"are caught between old and new ways of determining the
realities upon which moral values rest. In an age of rapid
intellectual change, they--and not they alone--confound
knowledge with knowledge."[58]

How, we may ask, does Ornstein's view differ from
the traditional critical view of Jacobean tragedy? To
answer this, however, a brief resumé of the traditional
view is necessary.

This older view sees the mainstream of Jacobean
tragedy as directly traceable to the bitter satires of Marston, especially his The Malcontent. Most of the tragedies
of the Jacobean period retain at least the formal shape of
the revenge play, which is traceable ultimately to Kyd's The
Spanish Tragedy. But revenge is a much subordinated theme
in these plays, and seldom does it show the simple blood-

for-blood motive of the early plays in the genre. Now the
motive may derive from other causes than murder, and more
than likely be born of malice rather than duty. The Jacobean
tragedy is concerned chiefly with the representation of vice
and sin, depicting more often than not the foulest possible
entanglements. Tragedy, like the drama generally after
1600, became less national in its scope, more inclined to be
critical, often in the most caustic terms, and less moral.
The spectacle of life in high places, at court in particular,
inspired little idealism among the serious dramatists, offering instead either objects for satire and cynicism or ultra-
sophisticated and courtly ideals of behavior. Unlike the
drama of the period before the turn of the century, tragedy
in this period was more skeptical about idealism and motivation and consquently less able to represent greatness of
mind. Jacobean drama was concerned primarily with the
analysis of abnormality and natural depravity which, without
a redemptive moral vision, often resulted in a shocking
failure of moral resolution. Thus, such a point of view
contends, tragedy came to be in the first decade of the
century merely a vehicle for the pandering of essentially
immoral sensationalism.[59]

Ornstein insists that such is not the case at all,
that a careful critical analysis of the works involved
illustrates a real philosophical concern for the eternal
verities of human experience such as courage, loyalty,

steadfastness, and idealism. Differing as they do in many
respects, the Jacobean tragedians are one in their contempt
for sham and hypocrisy, and in their constant probing the
appearances of things for a true reality. They probe merci-
lessly because they would find out what in the nature of man
or the universe man can ultimately depend upon. The explora-
tory operation is violent and traumatic, and more often than
not the patient fails to recover.

Ornstein is certainly right in rejecting the view
of Jacobean tragedy as decadent Elizabethan. And I believe
him to be correct in seeing Tillyard's view to be overly
simple, though I feel his criticism of Spencer to be only
partially true. My real objection to Ornstein's thesis,
however, has to do with its inapplicability to the tragedies of Webster, especially respecting the meaning of
the Machiavel figure. However true it may be in respect
to the tragedies of the other Jacobeans (including Shakespeare's perhaps, although I would largely disagree here
also), my conviction is that he is mistaken about Webster's.

Ornstein's approach to Jacobean tragedy is through
Chapman, and Chapman's is a philosophically oriented mind.
Webster, on the other hand, is the least philosophic of
poets. Whatever philosophic content there is in his
tragedy consists of what came along with the passages he
borrowed wholesale from his fellow poets and playwrights,
ancient and contemporary. To approach Webster's tragedy
by way of Chapman's tragic thought as Ornstein does is

seriously misleading, and Ornstein's treatment of the meaning
of the Machiavel figure in Webster's tragedies is the most
revealing case in point.

Ornstein treats the Machiavel figure more as convention than as seriously mythic, it seems to me. I do
not want to disagree with his treatment of what he calls
the pseudo-Machiavel, but simply to suggest a change of
emphasis respecting the meaning of this convention in
Webster's tragedy. Webster's choice of recent Italian history
as a source for his fictions, and the fact that he treats
both it and the Machiavel figure quite seriously, are revealing indeed, and Ornstein's approach does not allow for a full
appreciation of this. Ornstein is probably correct to reject
Theodore Spencer's thesis as oversimple; it yet remains true
that the Machiavellian material was ready to hand and imagina-
tively accessible when the divine right myth failed Webster
and those of his contemporaries who were also politically
oriented. The Machiavellian explanation suggested an only
too real possibility: that no human agency embodied the
wisdom and authority to curb the individual aspiring will.
The figure of the Machiavel and the setting of the Italian
Renaissance court offered an image of life at what the
Existentialists would call a frontier situation, the point
at which the individual may be tested in extremis. In
Webster's two great tragedies, the myth of the Machiavel
and his world is transformed and reshaped in such a way that
a truth with a universal validity about man and his world

emerges. To summarize: Just as Shakespeare employed the
Tudor myth for serious artistic purposes and ended by penetrating to a reality beyond it ("I think the king is but a man"),
so Webster accomplishes his radical re-evaluation of basic
Renaissance moral assumptions with the help of the
Machiavellian matter which was readily available to his hand,
and he too ends by penetrating through to a rejection of the
moral limitations imposed by such a vision of political man.

In his third and last tragedy, Appius and Virginia,
Webster moves away from the terrifying vision of the earlier
two tragedies toward a type of political quietism. Perhaps
this was inevitable in a writer so eclectic. Professor
R. W. Dent's excellent book on Webster makes it clear that
even in an age of heavy literary borrowing none was so in-
debted to his reading in general and his commonplace book
in particular as Webster.[60] An essentially non-analytic
thinker, he found the stuff of his tragedy in the political
dialectic of his age; and with the emergence of a new
political mythology after the period of moral confusion,
Webster appears to have reflected the new pieties. Appius
and Virginia, like Virgil's Aeneid, locates personal heroism
in self-denial and service to the community; and though in
both works the specific city is Rome, for Webster we
might read London. Such pious idealism, though probably
sincere on Webster's part, is antithetical to tragedy, since
tragedy, as I have been suggesting, has as a validating

condition a vision of irreconcilable values. Tragedy, according to R. J. Kaufmann, conducts an "ethical exploration" in
the process of which real and apparent necessities are
separated. It "tests the hero's competence in the face of what
is intractable in our natures, not merely in our political
situation."[61]

Notes to Chapter I

[1]For a brief but comprehensive account of the vogue
of Italian vice on the English Renaissance stage, see G. K.
Hunter, "English Folly and Italian Vice: the moral landscape of John Marston," Jacobean Theatre, Stratford-upon-
Avon Studies I, J. R. Brown & B. Harris, eds. (London,
1960), pp. 85-111.

[2]The Liberal Imagination (New York, 1950), pp. 20-21.

[3]Maynard Mack uses the phrase (p. 41) in "The
Jacobean Shakespeare: some observations on the construction
of the Tragedies," in Jacobean Theatre, Brown & Harris, eds.

[4]Lawrence Stone, "History a la Mode," The New York
Review of Books, III, No. 2, p. 7.

The quotation is from a wholly hostile review of a
recent book on the execution of King Charles by C. V.
Wedgewood, A Coffin for King Charles. Mr. Stone's detailed
rebuttal contains the following summary: "The reaction
[to the execution] was one of stunned passivity: not violent indignation against the deed and the doers of it, but
merely a resigned and thankful acceptance of the internal
peace which followed. Royalist risings had no support,
and the unstable regimes which followed in the next decade
collapsed more from internal dissension than the strength
of royalism" (p. 8).

[5]See in particular the late E. M. W. Tillyard's
most recent restatement of this material in Myth and the

English Mind (New York, 1962), Chapter 3, "Two Tudor Myths,"
pp. 42-59. And for a good summary application to Shakespeare's tragedy specifically, see William Rosen, Shakespeare and the Craft of Tragedy (Cambridge, 1960), pp. 1-3
and pp. 52-55.

[6]Few contemporary critics would be willing to describe King Lear in these terms, however, despite a similar
image of kingship (see Rosen on this last--pp. 1-3) and the
same approximate dating. Nor would I. Freed by its mythical
setting, Lear suggests a universe neither hostile nor
ordered, and certainly not benevolent. It is an indifferent
universe and evil is as boundless as man's own will. But
Lear, with Hamlet, stands at the beginning of the historical change I am here concerned with, and if Shakespeare's
greatest tragedy transcends his time, this is only what we
expect. Doubtless Macbeth, too, does, but not in the terms
I am arbitrarily imposing here. Thus most critics would
agree, I believe, that Macbeth is something of a philosophical anachronism in the evolution of Shakespeare's tragic
thought, insisting the while, however, on its validity as
popular theology (viz Rosen above). And since the popular
image is what I am concerned with, its definition in terms
of Macbeth is valid here.

For similar readings of Macbeth see H. C. Goddard,
The Meaning of Shakespeare, II (Chicago & London, 1951),
107-35; and Lionel Abel, Metatheater (New York, 1964).

38

[7]Bertrand de Jouvenel, On Power: Its Nature and
the History of Its Growth, trans. J. F. Huntington (Boston,
1962), pp. 17-35. For a history of the doctrine of divine
right, see J. N. Figgis, The Divine Right of Kings (Cambridge, 1896), and Studies of Political Thought from Gerson
to Grotius: 1414-1625 (New York, 1960).

[8]For a good summary treatment, see Robert Ornstein,
The Moral Vision of Jacobean Tragedy (Madison, 1960), p. 29
in particular.

[9]de Jouvenel, Chap. II, pp. 26-43, "Theories of
Sovereignty."

[10]de Jouvenel, p. 22. For a parallel in literary
criticism, Cf. Northrop Frye's concept of the "myth of
concern," which "exists to hold society together, so far as
words can help to do this. For it, truth and reality are
not directly connected with reasoning or evidence, but are
socially established. What is true, for concern, is what
society does and believes in response to authority, and a
belief, so far as a belief is verbalized, is a statement
of willingness to participate in a myth of concern." The
Critical Path: An Essay on the Social Context of Literary
Criticism (Bloomington & London, 1971), p. 36.

[11]p. 107.

[12]She characterizes the period from four or five
years before the death of Elizabeth to some five or six
years after the accession of James I as a period of

"despondency or anxiety." My interest for the most part will
be the early years of the reign of James, years during which,
Ellis-Fermor contends, "slackness of discipline, loss of
dignity and increase of expense combined to produce at once
dissatisfaction and a feeling of unsteadiness." The Jacobean
Drama (London, 1936), pp. 1-2.

[13]Modern historians tend to view the early years of
the seventeenth century as a period of transition from personal rule to parliamentary government, seeing James more as
victim than cause of the confusions and dislocations of his
time. Godfrey Davies writes that the tide of discontent
which was to reach its flood in the civil wars of the 1640's
"began to come in under James I." The Early Stuarts: 1603-
1660 (Oxford, 1937), p. xx.

[14]The personal unpopularity of the new sovereign
seems indeed to have contributed to the lowering of Court
standards. But more than this, his personality was especially unfitted to cope with the complex and peculiar issues
characteristic of a period in which the political keynote
was revolt against authority. (See Davis, p. xix.) The discontent of the middle classes with personal government grew
steadily, and the first decade of James's reign was characterized by the decay of older political forms and sanctions while few satisfactory substitutes were being devised.
Thus often enough loud protestations of divine sanctions
can best be understood as desperate attempts to bolster the

traditional political balance. But for obvious reasons
the seventeenth-century political commentary seldom shows
a concern with abstract historical and political forces;
they are, instead, personal and never dispassionate.

[15]For a theoretical treatment of the concept of
Authority, see Hannah Arendt, "What is Authority?" in
Between Past and Future: Six Exercises in Political Thought
(Cleveland and New York, 1963), pp. 91-141.

[16]Antony Weldon, Secret History of the Court of
King James I, 2 Vols., ed. by Sir Walter Scott (?), II
(London, 1811), p. 275.

[17]For a detailed account of this aristocracy, see
Paul N. Siegel, Shakespearean Tragedy and the Elizabethan
Compromise (New York, 1957).

[18]For the most comprehensive historical account of
this crisis of confidence in the authority of the aristocracy and its consequences for the belief in divine right
in England during our period, see Lawrence Stone, The Crisis
of the Aristocracy: 1558-1641 (Oxford, 1965).

[19]See Figgis, Political Thought from Gerson to
Grotius: 1414-1625, p. 98.

[20]The Myth of the State (Garden City, 1955),
p. 210.

[21]For a full and detailed treatment of the concept
of the generation, see José Ortega y Gasset, Man and Crisis,
trans. Mildred Adams (New York, 1958), pp. 30-101.

[22]Machiavelli was, after all, writing specifically about political man, and however much the "new science" may have contributed to a breakdown of the old, one doubts that "the destruction of the cosmos and the geometrization of space" (Alexandre Koyre, The Closed World to the Infinite Universe [Baltimore, 1957], p. viii) affected the popular imagination as much as, say, the latest royal scandal or the current taxation issues. But this has been discussed at length. I would like to add only the following as an example of what seems to me an appropriate statement of this issue: ". . . long before this change becomes visible in the methodology of the exact sciences, it announces itself in what might be called the new attitude and the new tone of the whole way of feeling the world." Ernst Cassirer, The Individual and the Cosmos in Renaissance Philosophy, trans. Mario Domandi (New York, 1963), p. 187.

For a good, detailed summary of the issues involved here, see Ornstein's Chapter I, "Tragedy and the Age," pp. 3-46.

[23]The Myth of the State, p. 174.

[24]For a detailed treatment of the characteristic method of Machiavelli as political teacher, see Leo Strauss, Thoughts on Machiavelli (Glencoe, Illinois, 1958).

[25]The Hero With a Thousand Faces (Cleveland and New York, 1956), p. 15.

[26]Leonardo Olachki, Machiavelli the Scientist (Berkeley, 1945), pp. 30-32.

[27]Strauss, pp. 290-94.

[28]P. 295.

[29]"To do justice to Machiavelli requires one to look forward from a pre-modern point of view toward an altogether unexpected and surprising Machiavelli who is new and strange, rather than to look backward from today toward a Machiavelli who has become old and our own, and therewith almost good. This procedure is required even for a purely historical understanding. Machiavelli did know pre-modern thought; it was before him. He could not have known the thought of the present time, which emerged as it were behind his back." (Strauss, p. 12)

[30]See L. C. Knights, Drama and Society in the Age of Jonson (London, 1937) for a detailed account of the socio-economic "background," and Ornstein, pp. 24-31, on the aspiring "new men."

[31]Ernst Cassirer, The Myth of the State, pp. 144-48. On the subject of the legendary versus the real Machiavelli, Cassirer writes:

> "It took a long time before this legendary picture of Machiavelli was overthrown. The philosophers of the 17th century were the first to attack that popular judgment. Bacon found in Machiavelli a kindred spirit; he saw in him the philosopher who had broken

away from all the scholastic methods and tried to study
politics according to empirical methods. 'We are much
beholden to Machiavelli and other writers of that class,'
says Bacon, 'who openly and unfeignedly declare or describe what men do, and not what they ought to do'"
(p. 148).

[32]For a most authoritative treatment of the connection between the man and his time, see Federico Chabod,
Machiavelli and the Renaissance, trans. David Moore (London,
1958).

[33]Shakespeare and the Nature of Man (New York, 1942),
p. 41.

[34]The Statecraft of Machiavelli (New York, 1962),
p. 55.

[35]The Myth of the Ruling Class: Gaetano Mosca and
the Elite (Ann Arbor, 1958), pp. 284-85.

[36]The Philosophy of Symbolic Forms, 3 vols., trans.
by Ralph Manheim (New Haven, 1953-57), II, 5. For an excellent historical treatment, see Felix Raab, The English
Face of Machiavelli, A Changing Interpretation, 1500-1700
(London, 1964).

[37]Myth critics such as Joseph Campbell, and more
recently, Northrop Frye, have treated this connection between cultural aspiration and the image of the hero in
literature extensively.

[38]"Myth and Identity," reprinted in Myth and
Myth-making, ed. H. A. Murry (New York, 1960), pp. 276-87.

Bruner is here describing the post-Freudian West; the phrase
and the general point, however, would apply equally to the
post-scientific early seventeenth century. See in particular Bruner's pp. 283-86.

[39]The Educated Imagination (Toronto, 1963), pp. 8-11.
For a more recent and considerably more comprehensive treatment of this concept, see Frye's The Critical Path, cited
above.

[40]See Hiram Haydn, The Counter-Renaissance (New
York, 1960), especially Chapter 7, "The Counter-Renaissance
and the Denial of Limit: The Naturalists," pp. 380-460.

[41]One thinks of T. S. Eliot's statement that "poetic originality is largely an original way of assembling
the most disparate and unlikely material to make a new
whole"; and Northrop Frye's critical theorizing about the
interaction of poetic sensibility and convention that characterizes the Shakespeare of the Sonnets, etc. See Frye's
"How True a Twain," Fables of Identity (New York, 1963),
pp. 88-106.

[42]Mark Schorer, "The Necessity of Myth," reprinted
as Appendix I, in Myth and Mythmaking, ed. Henry A. Murray
(New York, 1960), p. 355.

[43]Northrop Frye, Anatomy of Criticism (Princeton,
1957), pp. 283-84.

[44]Vernon Hall, Jr., Renaissance Literary Criticism
(Gloucester, Mass., 1959), pp. 174-76. See also W. Farnham,

The Medieval Heritage of Elizabethan Tragedy (Berkeley,
1936). During the nineteenth century the thematic and
formal influences on Elizabethan tragedy were exhaustively
detailed in such studies as John W. Cunliffe's The Influence
of Seneca on Elizabethan Tragedy (New York, 1893).

[45] Reprinted in J. W. Hebel & H. H. Hudson, eds.,
Poetry of the English Renaissance (New York, 1929), pp.
894-95.

[46] M. H. Abrams, The Mirror and the Lamp (New York,
1953). Not until the late eighteenth century does art
escape fully the control of the mirror figure, according
to Mr. Abrams, becoming from then on viewed chiefly as
"lamp," though often as both mirror and lamp. See also
mirror in index to Farnham's The Medieval Heritage of
Elizabethan Tragedy.

[47] The Idea of a Theater (Princeton, 1949), p. 14.
                    on
His chapter/Hamlet develops this idea at some length.

[48] Leonard F. Dean, "Richard II: The State and the
Image of the Theater," PMLA, Vol. 67, 1952, pp. 211-18.

[49] Political and Comic Characters of Shakespeare
(London, 1962), p. vii.

[50] Shakespeare's History Plays (Baltimore, 1962),
p. 10.

[51] Introduction, p. viii. More recent criticism
has added a corrective to what seems to me an oversimple
view here. See, for example, A. P. Rossiter, Angel with

Horns and Other Shakespeare Lectures, ed. Graham Storey

(New York, 1961), p. 59:

"Throughout the Histories it is in the implications of

the comic that shrewd, realistic thinking about men in

politics--in office--in war--in plot--is exposed: re-

alistic apprehension outrunning the medieval frame.

Because the Tudor myth system of Order, Degree, etc.

was too rigid, too black-and-white, too doctrinaire

and narrowly moral for Shakespeare's mind: it falsified

his fuller experience of men. Consequently, while em-

ploying it as FRAME, he had to undermine it, to qualify

it with equivocations: to vex its applications with

sly or subtle ambiguities: to cast doubts on its ul-

timate human validity, even in situations where its

principles seemed most completely applicable. His in-

tuition told him it was morally inadequate."

[52]Citations from Webster in my texts are to The Com-

plete Works of John Webster, ed. F. L. Lucas (London, 1928)--

hereafter cited as Works.

[53]The Human Image in Dramatic Literature (Garden

City, 1957), pp. 133-34.

[54]"E. M. W. Tillyard suggests that the Jacobeans were

able to write great tragedies because they had secure confi-

dence in humanistic ideals." He then quotes from Tillyard:

"Indeed all the violence of Elizabethan drama has nothing

to do with a dissolution of moral standards; on the contrary,

it can afford to indulge itself just because those standards

were so powerful. Men were bitter and thought the world
was in decay largely because they expected so much." The
Elizabethan World Picture (London, 1943), p. 18. "No one
can deny," continues Ornstein, "that the moral principles
of the age are high; but the question is whether the
tragedians believed that the principles did in fact govern
the conduct of men or express the reality of human conduct"
(Notes, p. 277).

Tillyard's position is supported, concerning the
validity of his account of an Elizabethan synthetic picture
of the world at any rate, by the following: A. O. Lovejoy,
The Great Chain of Being (Cambridge, 1936); and Theodore
Spencer, in Chapters I and II of Shakespeare and the Nature
of Man (New York, 1942), who notes at the very outset of
his work that "In the sixteenth century the combined
elements of Aristotelianism, Platonism, Neo-Platonism,
Stoicism, and Christianity were almost indistinguishably
woven into a pattern which was universally agreed upon,
and which, in its main outlines, was the same as that of
the Middle Ages" (p. 1).

[55]Spencer, Chapters I & II. For a more or less
general support of Spencer's hypothesis, see Victor Harris,
All Coherence Gone (Chicago, 1949); Michael Macklem, The
Anatomy of the World (Minneapolis, 1958); and in particular, Patrick Cruttwell's chapter on the intellectual background of what he calls the "Shakespearean Moment," in
The Shakespearean Moment (New York, 1960).

[56]Ornstein, p. 4.

[57]See especially Science and Religion in Elizabethan England (San Marino, 1953), where Paul H. Kocher according to Ornstein's note, "traces the development of natural science as a secular study and the acceptance before Bacon of the divorce of Scientific inquiry from religion (Chs. I and II). Mr. Kocher demonstrates conclusively that there was no general sense of conflict between religious and scientific truths in the late Elizabethan Age" (Notes, p. 278).

See also C. S. Lewis, The Discarded Image (Cambridge, 1964), on the whole subject of the impact of scientific thought on the imaginative model available to poets and artists:

"The Middle Ages, like most ages, were full of change and controversy. Schools of thought rose, contended, and fell. My account of what I call the Medieval Model ignores all this: ignores even the great change from a predominantly Platonic to a predominantly Aristotelian outlook and the direct conflict between Nominalists and Realists. It does so because these things, however important for the historian of thought, have hardly any effect on the literary level. The Model, as regards those elements in it which poets and artists could utilise, remained stable" (p. 13).

[58]Ornstein, p. 6.

[59]See for example Ashley H. Thorndike, Tragedy (Boston, 1908).

[60]*John Webster's Borrowing* (Berkeley, 1960).

[61]"The Seneca Perspective and the Shakespearean
Poetic," *Comparative Drama*, I, No. 3, p. 190. See also
Kaufmann's, "Tragedy and Its Validating Conditions,"
Comparative Drama, I, No. 1, pp. 3-18.

CHAPTER II

THE WHITE DEVIL

Despite an enormous amount of critical endeavor
the "tragic point," to use Northrop Frye's phrase, continues elusive in Webster's tragedies, especially The
White Devil. Yet critic and common reader alike attest to
the affective power of The White Devil and The Duchess of
Malfi, if not Appius and Virginia. In the case of The
White Devil, a major problem is the uncertain point of
view: "It is King Lear without both Lear and Edgar, the
protagonist for good."[1] To Professor Ellis-Fermor, however, a like uncertainty in Shakespeare's Troilus and
Cressida is a condition of that play's successful trans-
cendence of the limitations of dramatic form:

> The idea of chaos, of disjunction, of ultimate form-
> lessness and negation, has by a supreme act of artis-
> tic majesty been given form.[2]

Miss Ellis-Fermor finds the central question of Troilus
and Cressida to be "What is the nature of value and has
it or has it not an absolute existence?" The play's
artistic unity derives, she contends,

> not from an impression of balance, but from an impres-
> sion of evil enveloping apparent good; not from a pic-
> ture of the accidental prevalence of mischance and

injustice over wisdom and rectitude, but from the
implications of a causal relation between disjunction
in event and the absence of absolute criteria in the
universe of thought.

In spite of its being a dramatic tour de force, Miss Ellis-
Fermor finds the play unsatisfactory, since it lacks the
equilibrium of Shakespeare's later tragedies, "where the
positive element contends on equal terms with the negative
and the duality is essential in the artistic experience."[3]

My own reaction to Troilus and Cressida is simply
a lack of empathy. I can become involved intellectually,
but Shakespeare's irony keeps me detached from the characters and their fates, preventing anything more than an
intellectual response. If we assume that Troilus and
Cressida is defective as tragedy because of its excessive
irony, Professor Ellis-Fermor's point about the play's
lack of balance or equilibrium is interesting in quite a
different way from that which she intends. She is contending, actually, that tragedy be comprehensive in a way it
seldom if ever is. She is contending that tragedy must
tell the "whole truth"[4] about the human condition, and for
the reason that Shakespeare's later tragedies appear to her
to do exactly this. But tragedy, even Shakespeare's greatest, does not provide anything like the whole truth, nor
should we expect it to do so.

The fact that Webster's tragedies, <u>The White Devil</u>
especially, also lack the moral equilibrium Professor
Ellis-Fermor sees as a touchstone for determining great
tragedy has affected the critical judgments of even the
most perceptive and sympathetic of Webster's critics--
witness Clifford Leech:

> . . . when we see one of Shakespeare's major tragedies,
> we juxtapose the darkness of event with the light that
> could conceivably be, but in Webster there is no pos-
> sibility other than the one presented, there is no
> world imaginable but that of the fearful and the mad.[5]

What would seem to be needed, then, is an approach to Webster
which would make fewer comparisons of this kind with Shakespeare, recognizing not only that his vision is constricted
indeed as compared to Shakespeare's, but also that his tech-
nique and choice of sources were different from the greater
poet's. When he discovered about the nature of value and
the conflicting desires of men, he discovered by writing
poetry, and I suspect that Leech may indeed be correct in
his assertion that Webster "did not fully realize the significance of his plays."[6] We shall have to avoid treating
him as if he knew and, perhaps more important, as if his
stature in tragedy depended upon the comprehensiveness of
his view of human possibility rather than upon the intensity
of his vision and his considerable skill in realizing it
fully in his two important tragedies.

What about the tragic point in Webster then?
Tragedy has essentially to do with what Nietzsche called
the "will to power."[7] Typically, the hero elects to go
it alone and is destroyed as a consequence.[8] If he is a
person of significance, his action may bring chaos to an
entire society. The White Devil and The Duchess of Malfi
illustrate this paradigm surprisingly well. In the first,
Webster's focus is the political will-to-power and its
consequences for the hero and those who, for whatever
motives, share his vision; in the latter play, almost as
if he wished to explore the same situation from another
angle, the focus is not primarily the Machiavellian "intender"[9] but another type of hero, the victim of unbridled
political will. A victim may have tragic stature, however,
only insofar as there is this same quality of will. Ortega
describes the tragic hero as

. . . one who wants to be himself. The root of heroic
action may be found then in a real act of the will.
. . . The tragic figure is not tragic and therefore
not poetic, insofar as he is a man of flesh and blood,
but only insofar as he wills. The will, that para-
doxical object which begins in reality and ends in
the ideal, since one only wants what one is not--is
the tragic theme; and an epoch for which the will does
not exist, a deterministic and Darwinian epic, for
example, cannot be interested in tragedy.[10]

In Webster the world is conceived primarily in
political terms; and within the Machiavellian context,
politics is not only a purely secular activity, it is also
a sphere of action in which aspiring will may be shown and
tested.

2

We are introduced into the world of The White Devil
through the figure of Lodovico, an apparently conventional
revenger, who, we learn, has been forced by someone more
powerful than himself temporarily to suspend his customary
operations. Since the revenger is an established convention,
Webster needs only to sketch in the outline of Lodovico's
character and motive. Unlike the ghost of Machiavel returned
from the nether regions to provide melodramatic atmosphere
and motivation, Lodovico belongs to Webster's image of the
real world of the Italianate court. Lodovico's language is
appropriately melodramatic. Like the speech of Iago it is
certain of its categories and, given a particular environment, thoroughly conventional in its imagery, which is not
to suggest that such language is not dramatically effective.
Quite the contrary is true in fact. Its limitations are
Lodovico's own and, furthermore, they serve to characterize
an important segment of the world of the play, the narrowly
and humanly constricted reality of Renaissance Machiavellian
intrigue. However fantastic or distorted the particular

characters which flesh out the total image, such an image is
dramatically convincing if the characters are consistent
within that context. The world of the play, another way of
speaking of the playwright's vision of reality, is, after
all, merely the sum of the characters and the configurations
they assume as the fiction unfolds.[11]

As I noted above, Webster relies on Lodovico to serve
as a known quantity in this opening scene; but to read the
scene as simple melodrama, or as an example of blood-for-
blood tragedy, is to miss the central point. This is not
the simple matter of an attempt by Webster to refurbish the
Elizabethan revenge theme, but a relatively successful
exploiting of purely secular forces to provide the frame
of necessity and the sense of inevitability essential to the
tragedy. Unlike Greek tragedy, and plays such as Shakespeare's
Macbeth and The Winter's Tale, this play predicates no divine
redemptive force in the universe. Webster substitutes the
imperatives of a myth compounded of Machiavelli's simplistic
psychology and his secularized figure of Fortune.

What I have been saying suggests, I think, that a
primary attraction of the Italianate story of intrigue for
Webster was its capability to provide the essential sense
of causality, or logic, a tragedy must have. Certainly no
one would argue that what happens in The White Devil is just,
however inevitable it may very well seem to be. Lodovico
is important both to the plot, providing as he does an aspect

of the chain of causality, and to the tone and atmosphere of
this world. To define his role and how it fits into the
total image is therefore more important than his relative
unimportance as a character might at first suggest.

At first glance Lodovico would appear to have no
more dramatic function than his prototype, the Elizabethan
Machiavel, who, according to Robert Ornstein, has little
political significance outside of Shakespeare's and possibly
Marlowe's plays.

> His raison d'être is a primitive cynicism and aes-
> thetic appreciation of his own villainies. He has
> an instinctive appetite for horrendous crimes but
> only the vaguest interest in holding a sceptor. He
> is, in short, not a political subversive but an arch-
> enemy of the moral order, a "modern" representative
> of ancient evils, a diabolical incarnation of at least
> six of the Deadly Sins.[12]

In this first appearance Lodovico defines himself fully
and precisely, and Ornstein's description of the dramatic
function of his Elizabethan prototype would seem to apply
to him also--he is indeed mere primitive cynicism and aesthetic appreciation of his own villainies. What has changed
between Marlowe's Machiavel and Webster's is the moral order
imaged in the plays. Far from being an enemy of the moral
order, Lodovico is to become before the play is finished

the instrument of "moral" retribution. But what about the immediate dramatic impression and Lodovico's own perspective?[13]

In another context such a perspective would make Lodovico a comic character. Indeed, he comes close to being comic even in this context. Webster's strategy is to keep down his exposure time; the scene is short and extremely fast paced. The action bursts onto the stage and ends moments later with Lodovico's parting couplet, which summarizes all he knows of the ways of the world:

Great men sell sheep thus, to be cut in peeces,
When first they have shorne them bare and sold their
                       fleeces.

              (I, i, 61-62)

But this scene is a good deal more complicated than Lodovico's perspective alone would make it, since his simplistic view is but one element in the moral landscape of the play. Compared to Lodovico, Antonelli and Gasparo appear subtle indeed. Lodovico's response to their mocking banter is the bravado of the frustrated man of action. The rhythms and figures of his speech, as well as the contra-dictory particulars of his statements, all suggest this. Finally Antonelli offers him a bit of sententious advice to the effect that a little hardship will make him virtu-ous, or if not, will enable him to appear so. His response to this is to threaten revenge upon his still unspecified

enemies, when and if he returns. Gasparo's rejoinder ("O
Sir") I would take to be an expression of shock or, more
likely, feigned shock, at Lodovico's brutish failure of
decorum. The inference that seems inescapable here is
that Lodovico's banishment resulted more from his having
become something of a public scandal than from any particular crime or crimes he may be guilty of. Thus an important distinction is made very early in the play: that
appearances are all that really count.[14]

The next scene provides a distinct contrast to
the situation in scene one. Brachiano, in sharp contrast
to the banished Lodovico, is enjoying the best of good
fortune. The contrast is hardly to be missed. Lodovico
has referred to Brachiano's hoped for affair with Vittoria
explicitly and in some detail, and Brachiano's "Quite lost,
Flamineo," echoes Lodovico's opening "banisht!" rather neatly.
A most telling element in the contrast, however, is the visual
symbolism: Lodovico is depicted as an outcast; Brachiano is
introduced surrounded by all the appointments of power and
prestige--personal attendants, coaches, and all the light
and glitter of a splendid affair staged in his honor. As a
guide to the staging here, we might take the Cardinal's
word for the splendor of a Vittoria festivity:

. . . when severall night by night
Her gates were choak'd with coaches, and her roomes
Out-brav'd the stars with severall kind of lights,

When shee did counterfet a Princes Court,

In musicke banquets and most ryotous surfets. . . .

(III, ii, 75-79)

The host and hostess pass over the stage and
Flamineo and Brachiano are left alone together, during
which time Flamineo assures his master of success with
Vittoria, the object of his lust. Flamineo seems to me
what Ortega[15] would call a "spoiled utopian," the rational-
ist who goes further astray than anyone, since he is the
spectator who has lost confidence in his own point of view
and deserted his post. And in this respect he is clearly
related to the Malcontent figure of Marston. But since
Webster's purpose is not primarily satiric,[16] Flamineo cannot
be seen simply as a mouthpiece for the poet himself. The
irony, in other words, is Webster's and not Flamineo's own:
Unlike the Malcontent, who knows that experience is essential to knowledge, but who is himself disqualified from
participation in experience,[17] Flamineo's role makes him
an actual participant. His role is, therefore, perfectly
comprehensible as a role.[18]

He is here first of all because of his position in
the hierarchy of power. He is servant to Brachiano, and
Brachiano seeks to prostitute Vittoria. As brother to
Vittoria, Flamineo can arrange the affair. The terms of
this relationship are consistent with the relationships in
the play: all are subordinated within a rigid hierarchy

of power. As the narrative unfolds, we discover time and again that it is the power relationships that count.

We can get closer to the meaning of this play, therefore, if we put aside the notion that the evil figures are meant to be seen to "exist within a framework of good."[19] There are, to be sure, both good and evil figures in the play; but they exist side by side, so to speak, like the triumphant bull and the chaos of suffering humanity in Picasso's Guernica.[20] In the public world of Machiavellian politics, the world of the Italian Renaissance court as it appears in Webster, what is real and abiding appears to have more to do with the available roles to be played than with questions of good and evil. Hence the very real confusion of the seemingly clearsighted characters such as Flamineo. With no other controlling imperative but the momentarily expedient, the cynical opportunism of Flamineo and Vittoria and the limitless sentimentalism of the brutal Brachiano are inevitable.

3

In Webster and Renaissance drama generally we depend very significantly upon imagery to define character. And despite the impression we often get that character develops or changes in drama, the fact is that what we get is a successively refined definition of a mask, or persona.[21] Moreover, since a dramatic character is only

fully revealed in time, any discussion of character and
imagery must consider this fact. A character such as
Vittoria, for instance, will only be fully defined in the
course of the entire play,[22] while a relatively minor character such as the unfortunate Camillo may be defined at
once, in the space of a few minutes.

Related to this is the problem of how we are to
construe the meaning of particular scenes. To cite an
extreme instance of critical confusion, Irving Ribner's
study of Webster goes badly astray primarily because of
the way he approaches verbal imagery. Surveying the entire
play, he catalogues images into categories of good and evil,
and on the basis of this opposition, assigns meaning. Despite the fact that the good characters such as Cornelia
and Isabella are little more than hopeless spectators,
Ribner's reading serves to make of the play a conflict of
good and evil in the conventional sense.[23] Instead of
conflicting worlds of good and evil, it is more accurate to
see the central opposition in Webster's plays in terms of
power, struggles for ascendancy between characters who
recognize only force and who see morality only in terms of
masking, or role-playing; opposed to these are those who are
moral but helpless spectators. They are important because
they are moral and not because of the strength of their
opposition.

As I have suggested, the characterization of Camillo

is illustrative of Webster's craftsmanship. The playwright,
with any character, seeks a certain dramatic impression,
and in one sense the needs of this impression determine and
deploy the detail of characterization in any given situation.[24]
First of all then, what is recognizable in the figure of
Camillo? Flamineo has already said that Camillo is brain-
less and impotent; with the re-entry of Camillo, what follows is in part a demonstration of the truth of Flamineo's
description. Like Shakespeare's Polonius, Camillo loves
the extended figure, the sententious analogy. He picks up
the suggestive traveling of Flaminco and answers him
learnedly:

> FLA.   . . .--How now brother!--
> What, travailing to bed to your kind wife?
> CAM. I assure you brother no. My voyage lyes
> More northerlie, in a farre colder clime,
> I do not well remember I protest
> When I last lay with her.
>
>   (I, ii, 48-53)

Admitting his wife's contempt for him, he is led into the
extended figure of the bowling game. He would show his
knowledge of the world. Flamineo's bookish reply gives
him just the opportunity he wants; again he answers as
a would-be man of the world:

> CAM. Pew wew, Sir tell not me

Of planets nor of <u>Ephemerides</u>--

A man may be made Cocould in the day time

When the Stars eyes are out.

(I, ii, 73-76)

    Flamineo has little trouble in gulling Camillo.
He promises to patch the quarrel between Camillo and
Vittoria, making it seem as though Camillo has had no
hand in it. The truth of the matter, as Flamineo well
understands, is that Camillo is more interested in maintaining his pride than in sleeping with his wife.
Flamineo's obvious pleasure and exuberance in wooing his
sister for Duke Brachiano derives from the fact that in
wooing Vittoria he woos his own fortune. Camillo retires
to the rear of the stage, and Flamineo and Vittoria are
left alone in front. Pretending to work for Camillo,
Flamineo woos for Brachiano. In each of his major passages
he first addresses himself to Vittoria and Camillo; then,
in an aside to Vittoria (and the audience), he undercuts
what he has been saying about Camillo. Except to pick up
her cues, Vittoria remains silent throughout most of the
exchange. The imagery is especially interesting. Vittoria
is a "goodly foile," but Camillo "a conterfeite dyamond."
The contrast between Camillo and Brachiano is made quite
explicit: Brachiano will provide Vittoria with a ring
with a philosopher's stone in it. Camillo, thinking that
it is he who is spoken of responds with, "I am studying

alchemy." Thus Camillo takes Flamineo's metaphoric meaning and interprets it literally. (As in Marlowe's Doctor
Faustus, the images of alchemy suggest the transforming
of the world into one that will coincide with one's own
wishes.)

Actually, there are several points to be made about
the function of this exchange and Camillo's place in it. To
begin with, this display of Vittoria's impotent and foolish
husband, coming as it does before her seduction, serves to
soften her guilt. (The age and character of Camillo is
possibly one of Webster's major changes from his sources.[25])
But perhaps of more importance for Webster's intention is
the fact that Camillo's role here, egged on by Flamineo,
is that of a would-be politician, a parody of the real thing.
As we shall see momentarily, the various relationships throughout this scene, even the most intimate, are being structured
in the language and according to the doneès of power politics.

Camillo's wealth and his relationship with the
Cardinal have given him a way in to the world of court
intrigue, but his lack of vigor and his stupidity serve to
disqualify him as a successful politician, despite his
fondest wishes. From a "lousy slave" he has been raised up
to a certain eminence; however, incapable of adapting himself
to the needs of the moment, he will not enjoy Fortune's favors
for long. As a parody of the real politician he stands over
against Brachiano, who will fail not for reasons of stupidity

and lack of vigor, but rather because he will prove to be
mistaken, finally, about the nature of human relationships.
To Flamineo, Camillo stands in a more complex relationship:
Flamineo, too, would enjoy political power, and like
Camillo he is not of noble blood.

Since Camillo occupies a place in the hierarchy of
power, and as husband to Vittoria stands in the way of
Brachiano's and Vittoria's desires, he will reappear, if
only briefly, in a future context. His character has, however, already been fully revealed in this, his first appearance. There is no further development of Camillo's
character, either in terms of his personal perspective or
his place in the political scheme of things. Even murdered
he is pathetically unimportant, since no vendetta is
originated in his name.

In this scene the major characters grow in complexity, however, and in a manner which invites consideration
of the political implications. Already in thrall to Vittoria,
Brachiano is capable only of breathless questions about the
possibility of success with her. Flamineo, on the other
hand, having found out his path to preferment, is eager to
explain away any suggestion of possible failure. But lest
Brachiano get the idea that he might be able to succeed without
his good offices, Flamineo insists upon personally stage-
managing the scene throughout. Flamineo's vision of the
political is revealed almost at once: a position of power

makes the satisfaction of the appetites possible. Women
are "politic." They know that "desire is increas'd by the
difficulty of enjoying." The appetite for drink is increased by manipulating the supply at court:

> . . . --if the buttery-hatch at court stood continu-
> ally open there would nothing so passionate crowding,
> nor hot suit after the beverage,--
>
> (I, ii, 23-25)

Flamenco woos for Brachiano, and Vittoria is won
by such as this:

> Thou shaly lye in a bed stuft with turtles feathers,
> swoone in perfumed lynnen like the fellow was smothered
> in roses--so perfect shall be thy happinesse, that as
> men at Sea thinke land and trees and shippes go that
> way they go, so both heaven and earth shall seeme to
> go your voyage. Shalt meete him, tis fixt with nayles
> of dyamonds to inevitable necessitie.
>
> (I, ii, 148-53)

The sea voyage where appearance and reality become confused
is a major motif in the play. The first few lines of the
passage promise luxury, and the fact that Vittoria is convinced by this offers insight into her character. Flamineo's
sensual description of what Vittoria will gain from a liaison
with Brachiano is impressive indeed; but that such luxury

has associations of death is clear from Flamineo's analogy,
"like the fellow was smothered in roses." It is the irony
of the concluding image, which speaks of "nayles of dyamonds"
and "inevitable necessitie," however, which is most interesting. What Flamineo, the neophyte Machiavel, overlooks here
is that very element of unpredictability implicit in
Machiavelli's theory--where fortune and free will divide
human destiny, predictability is impossible.[26] In a
Machiavellian world of appearances, value judgments are difficult if not impossible.

Vittoria has been won; not by love but by promised
luxury. What we are interested to see now is what will
come of the expected lovemaking. Once the foolish Camillo
has been locked in for the night, Brachiano re-enters.
The imagery here is mostly of buying, selling, and promises
of luxury. Brachiano begins by asking for "credit."
Ironically, he associates the satisfaction of his lust with
eternal salvation:

> BRA. Give credit: I could wish time would stand still
> And never end this entervew, this hower,
> But all delight doth it selfe soon's devour.
> Let me into your bosome happy Ladie,
> Powre out in stead of eloquence my vowes--
> Loose me not Madam, for if you forgoe me
> I am lost eternallie.
>   (I, ii, 192-98)

Vittoria gives as good as she gets. Brachiano has just referred to her as "a sweet phisition." Mocking the courtly love tradition, her reply brings together the cruel lady of convention with doctors, funerals, and "credit."[27]

During this intimate exchange, already watched by both Flamineo and Zanche,[28] the horrified Cornelia enters from behind; her aside passes moral judgment upon all the participants:

My feares are falne upon me, oh my heart!
My sonne the pandar: now I find our house
Sinking to ruine. Earth-quakes leave behind,
Where they have tyrannised, iron, or lead, or stone,
But woe to ruine, violent lust leaves none.

(I, ii, 206-10)

Thus the seduction scene is a dramatization of the conventional Jacobean body-soul debate. Webster's dramatic strategy is to objectify the conflict in terms of several characters, each of whom makes concrete a particular fragment, thereby anatomizing the whole into a series of roles. And this is true for the play generally: the particulars of a conflict are pretty much taken for granted--we are told in the first scene, for instance, about Brachiano's design to seduce Vittoria. Unlike many of Shakespeare's characters, Webster's do not tease us by suggesting depths of personality unrevealed. What is dramatized is the revelation of particular

destinies. Or, to state it another way, the emphasis is on
the consequences of certain actions rather than on the
particular motivations.

And thus the importance of recognizing just how much
of a commonplace the body-soul debate, and its expression in
the opposition of love and lust, had become by 1612. Illustrations from Shakespeare come immediately to mind, but
almost any contemporary might offer as many. Sonnet 129,
for instance, or this passage from Venus and Adonis:

"Call it not love, for Love to heaven is fled,
Since sweating Lust on earth usurp'd his name;
Under whose simple semblance he hath fed
Upon fresh beauty, blotting it with blame;
    Which the hot tyrant stains and soon bereaves,
    As caterpillars do the tender leaves.

"Love comforteth like sunshine after rain,
But Lust's effect is tempest after sun;
Love's gentle spring doth always fresh remain,
Lust's winter comes ere summer half be done;
    Love surfeits not, Lust like a glutton dies;
    Love is all truth, Lust full of forged lies."
                                    (793-804)

Webster could expect from his contemporary audience a clear
recognition of the moral issues involved here, and perhaps
fully as important, he could expect the audience to come to

a conclusion similar to that of Cornelia--that inevitable
consequences must follow from such conduct. This moral
perspective is essential to the play, since the distance
between the normal and conventional--Cornelia, Marcello, etc.--
and the extreme represented by Brachiano is an important
measure of Webster's meaning.

It is the playwright's diction, however, which offers
the best insight into his meaning. The entire bargain is
structured in political terms--witness Brachiano's reply to
Vittoria's fears:

. . .

You are lodged within his armes who shall protect you,

From all the feavers of a jealous husband,

From the poore envy of our flegmaticke Dutchesse--

I'le seate you above law and above scandall,

Give to your thoughts the invention of delight

And the fruition; nor shall government

Divide me from you longer than a care

To keepe you great: you shall to me at once,

Be Dukedome, health, wife, children, friends and all.

(I, ii, 250-58)

And even Cornelia's protest emphasizes public rather than
private honor:

The lives of Princes should like dyals move,

Whose regular example is so strong,

They make the times by them go right or wrong.

(I, ii, 270-81)

What she is saying is obvious: it is doubly damnable for a prince to be immoral since so much depends upon his right example. And as if to prove her correct, the remainder of the scene is a dramatization of the effect of a corrupt court· upon the character of Flamineo.

Webster's dramatic skill in the remainder of this scene is impressive indeed. Instead of fulfilling our expectation regarding the outcome of the Vittoria-Brachiano affair, he holds that in abeyance by having Flamineo absorb, so to speak, the center of interest. By the time that Flamineo's harsh cynicism to his mother drives her from the stage in misery the spectator is fully apprised of the cost of such near-sighted wisdom as Flamineo's Machiavellian kind. But the spectator learns also the price to a spirit such as Flamineo's of avoiding involvement with the world of the court. If those who gravitate to the center of power are inevitably corrupted, those who resist the lure must be satisfied to remain forever impotent and insignificant. Thus the insistent paradox that haunts Webster: how to reconcile an absolute moral imperative with the realities of political power as he visualized them. It would be difficult to construe the very real passion and bitterness of Flamineo's protest to his mother in any other terms--

. . .

    I would faine know where lies the masse of wealth

    Which you have whoorded for my maintenance,

    That I may beare my beard out of the levell

    Of my Lords Stirop.

                    (I, ii, 305-308)

          . . . Conspiring with a beard

    Made me a Graduate--then to this Dukes service--

    I visited the Court, whence I return'd

    More courteous, more letcherous by farre,

    But not a suite the richer; and shall I,

    Having a path so open and so free

    To my preferment still retaine your milke

    In my pale forehead? . . .

                    (I, ii, 316-23)

In the eyes of such as Flamineo, the world has been contracted to the limits of the court, a sphere of action most easily understood in Machiavellian terms. To achieve glory, or immortal renown, a man needs both virtù and fortune. Virtù has nothing to do with Dante's usage, or with the English <u>virtue</u>. It means, rather, "manliness," and it is essentially amoral. Both glory and fortune designate purely secular concepts, and it is this secular- ized image of Fortune (as opposed to Dante's religious image) that provides the combination of freedom and necessity the tragedy requires. The plastic and intellectual unity

of Dante's image of Fortune--an image that forced all opposing themes into one great synthesis, making of it an entity
with its own character but at the same time locating it
within the spiritual and divine cosmos--is gone forever by
Webster's day, never to be achieved again. But this loss
also signifies a new liberation. In the medieval doctrine
of two worlds, man is at the mercy of the forces that are
fighting over him. He simply stands apart, a spectator.
Ernst Cassirer describes the difference in terms of man's
relationship to his world: Though man

> experiences the conflict of these forces, he takes
> no active part in it. He is the stage of this great
> drama of the world, but he has not yet become a truly
> independent antagonist. In the Renaissance a different
> image emerges ever more clearly. The old image of
> Fortune with a wheel, seizing men and dragging them
> along, sometimes raising them, sometimes throwing them
> down into the abyss, now gives way to the depiction
> of Fortune with a sailboat. And this bark is not con-
> trolled by Fortune alone--man himself is steering it.
> . . . the statements of the theoreticians point
> in the same direction. This is especially true of those
> theoreticians concerned with a definite sphere of action
> or creation rather than scholastic knowledge. For
> Machiavelli, Fortune rules over half of all human
> actions. But she gives herself to him who acts, to

him who quickly and boldly grasps her, and not to the
passive observer.[29]

If it is true that power is the chief reality in
the world of The White Devil, then a major contrast in
the play is that between those in power and those out of
power, the world of masters and that of slaves. The only
escape to being "a lousy slave" (Flamineo's term for what
Camillo was before he came to preferment) is to possess
enough power to realize one's own dreams of self-aggrandizement. Power enables one to reshape the world to one's own
pleasure. So long as Duke Brachiano is willing to stay
at home, husband to Isabella, who is sister to Francisco,
the Grand Duke of Florence, his position in the hierarchy
is secure.

Once we have begun to see the play in these terms,
moreover, many of the heretofore puzzling characters and
relationships begin to seem less confusing: Thus the fate
of the banished Lodovico--a "decay'd" Count, his power has
drained away with his wealth. Incapable of curbing his
appetites, he has suffered the consequence of being unable
to play the fox, punishment at the hand of someone more
powerful than himself. This makes dramatic sense of Webster's
use of the conventional body-soul opposition in the relatively unconventional political context, where the conflict
seems not to take place within the protagonists but among
them. And thus Flamineo's passion for policy and Brachiano's

curious diction even in love-making. With Webster as with
no other of his contemporaries--especially Shakespeare,
perhaps--it is really impossible to separate a character
from his context. Less than individual character and motivation, Webster's primary interest is the particular type
and his place in and effect upon the various relationships
that bind men together in society.

4

In structure Webster's tragedies differ significantly from Shakespeare's, with the possible exception of
Lear. As in Lear, the focus of attention in The White
Devil and The Duchess is not so much the individual character as the social unit itself. And if we understand
that Webster's chief interests are best served by his own
kind of dramaturgy--the creation of a sequence of confrontations, in which often enough one or more characters will
be "out of character"--we will come close to understanding
what he is about. The fact of the matter is, moreover,
that the individual scene in Webster is so skilfully made,
and so effective as drama, that questions of plot and consistency simply do not occur unless one's approach has been
influenced by expectations derived from other kinds of
plays.[30]

With Act II, Scene i, Webster begins to modify the
images of Act I, where character and relationship are

construed exclusively in terms of success or failure in a
context of power. And as we have seen, it is the characters
themselves who determine this configuration.

The dramatic impression created by scenes such as
Act II, Scene i significantly modify the image of power as
the ultimate social reality. Not that the idea that
political success is dependent upon ruthlessness and the
employment of Machiavellian principles is refuted; it is,
rather, modified in such a manner as to suggest that things
are, indeed not so simple as all that. There is, in other
words, no conceptualized denial of Machiavellian reality,
but rather an image of man in society which places the
Machiavellian in a slightly different context. What
Webster is suggesting here is that his Machiavellians are
mistaken in their assumption that men are in society only
by accident or artifice. Natural impulse has its reality
and its own power to shape the world. Given an appropriate
climate, love and simple affection also exert powerful
demands.

Webster's presentation in this scene is anything
but simple, however, since he has chosen to present
Brachiano's opposition, the politically entrenched Monticelso
and Francisco de Medicis, in a context which is at once
familial, religious, and political. What emerges is, on
the one hand, an image of what Brachiano stands to lose by
his lawless course of action, and on the other, a political

parable of why. As the world depicted in the play grows
ever more complex, so the area of actual freedom available
to the characters diminishes. Although this fact becomes
increasingly more clear to the reader, or spectator, the
characters themselves are of course unaware, until they
actually confront death, of how little freedom of action
they have. One reason we find Giovanni's hopeful speech
at the close of the action perfunctory at best is the
recognition we share with the protagonists, however briefly,
that even in a better world there is precious little real
freedom of action available to the individual.[31]

By the end of Act II, then, despite the murder
and intrigue, we are aware of an action far more complex
than a melodramatic opposition of Machiavellian antagonists.
Before taking up the question of what such a world means in
terms of the characters and their roles, it might be useful
to ask specifically how much freedom of action each of the
characters has, and has had from the first.

Despite the illusion of freedom enjoyed by Brachiano
and his followers, they have from the first had little freedom in actuality. We have seen that the tragic hero is one
who would shape the world to his own pleasure, regardless
of the consequences. By the end of Act III, however,
Brachiano and Vittoria go the way of Lodovico, who was
banished from Rome in the opening scene of Act I. The lovers
still entertain the illusion of freedom, but we are aware of

just how illusory this is. With Flamineo, perhaps the most
misled of all, they have felt that they possessed the freedom to dispose of troublesome people who got in their way--
specifically a husband, a wife, and in the case of Flamineo,
a brother. The freedoms they seize upon--to use others in
the belief that they thereby enlarge their own freedoms--
prove finally to be illusory, and our awareness of this is
a function of Webster's superb control of dramatic irony.

To be specific, what are some of the important
ironic parallels and recognitions of the play? Brachiano
promises to protect Vittoria and to make Flamineo's fortune;
ultimately he cannot protect even himself in the security of
his own court. Cornelia, from the best of motives, cannot
protect her daughter's honor, nor even the lives of her
sons, one of whom is the soul of honor. When Marcello is
killed by Flamineo she attempts futilely to protect the
fratricide. With the opening of Act V, the major characters
have almost no freedom of action; ironically, however, they
exult in what they believe to be the achievement of total
freedom; Flamineo welcomes this new day:

In all the weary minutes of my life,
Day nere broke up till now. This mariage
Confirmes me happy.
(V, i, 1-3)

They have succeeded temporarily at least in recasting the
world to the image of their own pleasures. Their wish-

fulfillment dreams have, they believe, been realized, and
now all that remains is the enjoying of them.

Webster is leading his audience to an understanding
of what is, and what is not, possible in this world. The
wedding scene of ritual pomp and circumstance is itself
ironic: the same Ambassadors who lent their collective
dignity to the Act III trial scene are in attendance for
the wedding ceremony of Brachiano and Vittoria. The
ironies proliferate, for we know what the protagonists
cannot know.

New arrivals are welcomed to Brachiano's court--
the disguised Francisco and his fellow conspirators. There
is much talk of the vanity of human wishes and a great
deal of moralizing on princes and power, especially between
the disguised Francisco, the cynical Flamineo, and his
brother, Marcello.[32] What is important here is not the
conventional moralizing but that each of them defines the
world differently, and characteristically. (Francisco's
definition of the world is characteristic in terms of his
assumed role, that of the idealistic soldier of his
disguise, Mulinassar.) Flamineo forces his brother Marcello
into silence by making him admit that he has done "poorly"
as a soldier. For Mulinassar, Flamineo has some "polliticke
instruction":

              . . . The Duke saies hee will give
   you pension; that's but bare promise: get it under his

hand. For I have knowne men that have come from serving against the Turks; for three or foure moneths they
have had pension to buy them new wodden legges and
fresh plaisters; but after 'twas not to bee had. And
this miserable curtesie shewes, as if a Tormenter
should give hot cordiall drinkes to one three quarters
dead o' th' racke, onely to fetch the miserable soule
againe to indure more dogdaies.

(V, i, 130-38)

And a few lines later, he describes his love affair with
Zanche in the following terms:

> . . . I doe love that Moore, that
> Witch very constrainedly: shee knowes some of my vil-
> lanny; I do love her, just as a man holds a wolfe by
> the eares. But for feare of turning upon mee, and
> pulling out my throate, I would let her go to the
> Devill.

(V, i, 147-51)

Taking all of these passages together, especially
in the context of the action which follows, the dramatic
point is clearly that these persons all are fated to live
in a world of their own definition. The torrent of action
which concludes with the carnage in the final scene seems
to bear this out. Brachiano, for instance, dies horribly
in isolation, surrounded by his enemies; and with the death

of Brachiano, Vittoria's recognition comes about:·

O mee! this place is hell.

(V, iii, 182)

And this place is hell. Murderers disguised as monks chant
the Latin rites of the dead over their victim. The mad
Cornelia sings over the body of her son, murdered by his
brother. Francisco has indeed stirred up hell. But the
Satanic parody into which the action plunges is not to
be explained simply in terms of the deus ex machina of
Francisco's revenge. This "descent" was prefigured from
the first, present from the opening lines of the first
scene, in both the imagery and the implications of perspective and action.

What is the essential difference between the
Jacobean and the Elizabethan view of politics, however?
Webster's world, like that of Jonson's in Volpone for instance,
is often described as a fallen world. Still primarily
Christian, his cosmology is assumed to be like the earlier
medieval-renaissance one, only more gloomy. Critics of
this persuasion cite the language of the play, which does
indeed reflect most of the older Christian world view.[33]
Such references, however, are inevitable, since the language
of the tribe, to use Eliot's phrase, had been shaped by
centuries of Christianity by the seventeenth century.

The cosmology of The White Devil, unlike that of
Macbeth, for instance, is curiously truncated. The old

three- or four-fold division of the universe is either
gone entirely or become a faint echo. The old cosmology
has been collapsed, so to speak. Heaven is far away, having little immediate reality for mankind, and "hell" is
here. This hell is not necessarily a consequence of sin,
but rather of an inability to locate some touchstone of
true value. What the world of the play offers, then, is
the old levels of man and Nature telescoped. And much of
the confusion about Webster's meaning can be traced, I
believe, to the fact that he is still attempting to work
out these concepts himself. If we assume that Webster is
picturing the secular world as all there is, thus making
a human-centered system of values essential to human hap-
piness, some of these problems become less difficult.
All of the "testing," for instance, wherein characters
like Flamineo perversely insist upon applying the acid
test to everything, can be seen to have some relevance.
In such a world even success is a joyless achievement,
which accounts for the vision of unrelieved gloom that
Leech and others have complained of in Webster's plays.[34]

5

The images of chaos presented in the final scene
of The White Devil points up the immense gap between the
various characters' axpectations and what actually is.
And since the play demonstrated early on the impotence of the

morally good, it is those who are indifferent or antag-
onistic to morality who aspire and act. Anyone may mis-
construe the nature of reality, but only the hero miscon-
strues it grandly, immensely. Thus the intensity of a
character's commitment to his dreams of self-aggrandizement
is a measure of the tragic irony involved in his fall, for
the more intense a character's sense of self the greater
the gap between what is and what he desires. It is the
struggle a character makes, the intensity of his suffering,
that fascinates us and evokes pity; just as it is the
inevitability of his destruction that terrifies. This
brings me to what is central in Webster, as it must be in
the work of every tragic poet, the place of suffering and
its consequence for character.

The Act III trial scene seems to me a microcosm
for the world of the play, including as it does both an
image of Vittoria at her most intensely committed, and an
anatomy of the humanly tortuous Italianate court. Like
other of his heroines, Vittoria insists upon being herself
in the face of immense pressures, and oddly enough, she is
most intensely "alive" when she is playing the role of
injured innocence, betrayed lover, or naive but gay com-
panion. Simply to assert that from the Machiavellian perspective social reality is the playing of roles does little
to explain the impression she conveys in the Act III trial
scene. The conflict is between reality as conceived from

the conventional point of view--religious, legal, moral--
and reality as conceived from Vittoria's individual perspective, her sense of felt life.

We are familiar with the way trial by combat func-
tioned in the still medieval setting of Shakespeare's
Richard II, and how such a scene could become a measure
of the dislocation between appearance and reality, as the
trial by combat scene is in that play.[35] At a later period
in history, the court of law came to take the place of
trial by combat; the function, however, remained essentially
the same, that of a ritualized mode for the accomplishment
of justice which would minimize the danger to the public
weal in settling private quarrels. Thus the two scenes can
be seen to serve roughly analogous functions within their
differing contexts. (When law court scenes in Webster and
Shakespeare are compared, interestingly enough, justice is
always seen to be at fault in Webster and almost never in
Shakespeare.)[36]

What both playwrights obviously well understood is
that a court trial scene may be used to characterize a
society as well as a particular defendant or other participant in the trial itself. Webster pushes this a step
further by making use of the fact of Brachiano's exclusion
from the court proceedings in a functional manner.
Brachiano's willingness to scorn appearances is emphasized
by his showing up in person where no place has been provided
for him. There is no place for Brachiano, according to the

Cardinal, because the Pope himself has left the business to him. The truth of the matter is, as we already know, that it is actually Brachiano who is aimed at, despite Vittoria's being the one who is on trial. His refusal to respect decorum makes him an outsider, and the fact that he even appears in the court is a measure of his personal commitment to Vittoria and his fatal course of action.

Both the lack of real evidence and the fact that this is a Church trial help to explain the mechanics of the proceeding itself. Vittoria has little difficulty in defeating the lawyers, but the Cardinal is more formidable. The "character" he paints in the process of affixing the role of whore on Vittoria is impressive indeed. Vittoria's response is to reject the role outright, to assert her personal identity. And thus it is that the imagery of the scene, paradoxically, shows it to be a contest between natural impulse on the one hand, and a rigid and constricting authority on the other.

As I have been suggesting, Vittoria asserts what she feels to be her natural identity against the role assigned to her by the court. Unlike the identity a person feels to be true for himself, which is based on the world of sensation that gives him a sense of organic coherence, a role tends to define an individual not as an entity enduring in time, but by what he has done in particular instances. And as in the case of a courtroom trial, corrupt or otherwise,

the concepts of conventional morality or social awe 'end to
define an individual in terms which have nothing to do with
his own felt reality.[37] Such may be true of other conventions besides the law court--witness, for instance, the
confusion which results when Hamlet rejects the role of
revenger assigned to him by the ghost. Vittoria's trial has
the effect of violently juxtaposing assigned role and
personality, and on a public "stage." The fact that she
refuses to the very end the role the Cardinal and the court
attempt to impose, insisting that justice has been "raped,"
is an important recognition for both her character and the
plot. Having proved little against her beyond a lapse of
public decorum, the Cardinal is reduced to pleading "the
condition of the present time," which is of course a kind
of last resort for the exertion of naked force.[38]

Vittoria, paradoxically, wins a moral victory; and
the tenuous balance between individual will and public
"necessity" is thrown off even further when she is packed
off to the house of convertites. We are certain that she
will reject the role of convert, just as she has rejected
the role of public sinner. It is thus that we understand
her concluding passage:

It shal not be a house of convertites--
My minde shall make it honester to mee
Then the Popes Pallace, and more peaceable
Then thy soule, though thou art a Cardinall--

Know this, and let it somewhat raise your spight,

Through darkenesse Diamonds spred their ritchest light.

(III, ii, 300-305)

So much for her public presence; but what can we infer from the totality of what we know by now about her place in the political configuration?

Vittoria is circumscribed respecting her political potential by the limitations of her sex. Because she is a woman in a patristic society, the sphere of direct political action is outside her natural limits. Yet she is a protagonist in what is essentially a tragedy of politics. She has willfully inserted herself into the world of power, which is, of course, the world of the play itself. In addition to the limitations imposed upon her by sex, Vittoria is at the start of the play without the legitimacy which comes with noble birth or is acquired through noble marriage. Her marriage to Camillo brings her wealth enough to satisfy her social aspirations. But she has been disappointed in her marriage in an area other than Camillo's sexual incompetence: Camillo's pedigree is unpromising indeed. His political aspirations are, as we have seen, mere clownish pretension, and perhaps worst of all, the men of real power all hold him in contempt, even to Monticelso, whose nephew he is. Camillo is wealthy and stupid, which gives Vittoria the lebensraum she needs

socially; and according to the charges brought against her
at her trial, she has achieved a good deal of success. But
Camillo's relationship to the Cardinal seems not to have
been very fruitful. Monticelso's power, before he becomes
Pope at any rate, seems severely circumscribed. He is
fearful of offending Brachiano, and until the actual murder
of Camillo, when vengeance becomes a matter of family honor,
he shows only scorn and contempt for his luckless cousin.
The relationship has obviously been no source of joy to him.
(Camillo murdered is something else again, a circumstance
both Vittoria and Brachiano seem careless of in their
intrigue.) Vittoria, wishing to realize her aspirations,
has looked to Brachiano for a champion. The very nature of
her hold upon him, however, the sexual thralldom which
motivates his ruthlessness in murder and intrigue, serves
also to disable him in the political arena, where appearances are essential.

But to return to the Act III trial scene. Like any
ceremonial occasion, the trial scene provides more than
simply courtroom drama. For one thing, it provides a
"stage" for the acting out of certain roles, and thus an
anatomy of the particular society. We are made to see just
how much freedom--and justice--is available to the individual. For another, the ceremonial occasion brings the
characters of the play together into a group with a common
purpose and intent, thereby putting concerns of a strictly
personal and private kind temporarily aside. The heroic

characters refuse to participate according to the rules, however, and because justice itself is being manipulated here--the Cardinal is bot h judge and prosecutor--we are made intensely aware of the failure of authority, despite the fact that the stage-managers have supplied all the stage properties of respected hierarchy.

Where role-playing is indulged by one and all, any kind of intense commitment must be a liability. But this does not mean that the simply conventional are safe either, for in a society without a standard of justice--in Webster this means a ruler of absolute moral authority--no one is safe, and only the fools and simple-minded are without fear. The Act III court trial closes on a chaos that prefigures the far more terrifying chaos of the final scenes of the play.

After the trial Vittoria, Flaminco, and Brachiano are safe for the moment, but the testing of their characters is to continue to the very moment of death. It is the death scene of Vittoria and Flamineo which illustrates best the symbolic significance of the role-playing of Webster's heroes and heroines. Only in the face of death itself do they finally exhaust the available possible roles; it is then that the essential (or existential) personal reality may at last be revealed. (Flamineo even acts out a symbolic death and rebirth before his actual death in the final scene of Act V.) And all of this role-playing helps to

explain why we are never quite certain, afterwards, whether
we have been fooled--there is always the possibility that
courage is, after all, only a question of showmanship.
Whatever reservations we may have about Flamineo, however,
I believe Clifford Leech is correct in his assessment of
Vittoria's courage in the face of death:

> Hope is gone after that [Vittoria's failure to win
> Lodovico with flattery], and she is the stronger for
> it. She taunts her murderers, and denies that she
> will tremble or look pale with fear. There is an
> authority in her last words that has fixed them in
> every reader's memory. For the first time there is
> a genuine expression of remorse: "O my greatest
> sinne lay in my blood, Now my blood paies for't"--
> remorse accompanied by a stoical acceptance are the
> children, not of faith, but of dark uncertainty.
> . . . Finally, at the moment of death, Vittoria
> blames her guilt on the corruption of Courts. . . .[39]

Institutionalized controls such as the law and
religion are disqualified by their own corruption, or
clearly inadequate to curb the lawless will. Viewed from
this perspective, the central theme of the play would seem
to be how may a purely secular and all-too-human society
reconcile these mighty opposites, individual will and the
ideal of justice. Webster continues his search in The

Duchess of Malfi, and in Appius and Virginia [40] he apparently
resolves the paradox, with what result we shall examine.

Notes to Chapter II

[1]Gunnar Boklund, The Sources of the White Devil,
Essays and Studies on English Language and Literature XVII
(Uppsala, 1957), p. 184. See also Travis Bogard, The
Tragic Satire of John Webster (Berkeley, 1955), pp. 38-44,
for a contrast between the characterization of Shakespeare
and that of Webster. Bogard goes on to argue, however,
that since we cannot locate the tragic element in any
single character, as in Shakespearean tragedy, what we
have is a tragedy of society, hence "tragic satire," which
seems to me a contradiction in terms. The distinction
here is the relatively commonplace one, that the satiric
presupposes both a certain moral frame of reference and
a desire to reform, thereby eschewing the intense question-
ing of received values and the profound sense of moral
ambiguity we have come to associate with the tragic mode.
Jonson, I would argue, wrote his two Roman "tragedies" in
a satiric mode precisely because, morally speaking, he
always knew what he knew.

[2]The Frontiers of Drama (New York, 1946), p. 72.

[3]P. 69.

[4]The phrase is Aldous Huxley's. For his discussion of the concept in literature generally, see "Tragedy
and the Whole Truth," Collected Essays (New York, 1958),
pp. 96-103.

[5]John Webster: A Critical Study (London, 1951),
p. 31.

[6]P. 32.

[7]Northrop Frye describes it thus: ". . . for the theory of tragedy one naturally looks to the psychology of the will to power, as expounded in Adler and Nietzsche. Here one finds a 'Dionysiac' aggressive will, intoxicated by dreams of its own omnipotence, impinging upon an 'Apollonian' sense of external and immovable order." Anatomy of Criticism, pp. 62-63.

[8]Cf. Albert Cook, The Dark Voyage and the Golden Mean: A Philosophy of Comedy (Cambridge, 1949), who writes: "When one man, seeking pleasurable experience and not profound wisdom, leaves the groove of the probable, he disturbs for evil the whole society, especially in its smallest unit, the family" (p. 24).

[9]The term "intender" is used by the political theorist Bertrand de Jouvenal to denote the opposite of "attender," making roughly the same distinction as "politician" vs. "statesman." The Pure Theory of Politics (New Haven, 1963), pp. 169-75.

[10]José Ortega y Gasset, Meditations on Quixote (New York, 1961), p. 152.

In the case of Brachiano, an impassioned will finds its object in Vittoria. For the Jacobean, will meant also lust, as in Shakespeare's Sonnet 135. In the case of Vittoria, and the Duchess of Malfi also, will is expressed as an attempt to live according to her own felt reality.

[11]See Arthur Sewell, Character and Society in
Shakespeare (London, 1951), for a concise statement of
this concept:

> ". . . in Shakespeare's mature plays even a minor char-
> acter will enrich, diversify, and individually quicken
> the comprehensive view. Of that view he is the product,
> but in that view he is also an agent. . . . In him, as
> in a single brush-stroke in a picture, a moment of vi-
> sion, a new angle of attitude, transforms to however
> small an extent, and lights up, the whole matter" (p.
> 20).

[12]The Moral Vision of Jacobean Tragedy (Madison,
1960), p. 25.

[13]For a discussion of "perception," or "point of
view," in drama, see Leonard F. Dean's Introduction to
his translation of The Praise of Folly by Desiderius
Erasmus (New York, 1946), p. 21:

> "Erasmian irony . . . produces a meaning comparable
> to that derived from a play or from any piece of lit-
> erature conceived as drama. The irony is composed
> of the simultaneous expression of several points of
> view, just as a play is composed of speeches by many
> different characters; and the meaning of the irony
> and of the play is not that of any one point of view
> or of any one character, but of all of them interact-
> ing upon each other. The result is not paralysis or

abject relativism, but a larger truth than that presented by any one of the elements alone."

[14] Leech concludes his discussion of this scene as
follows:

"This first scene with Lodovico strikes the keynote
for the play. Here is a man given over to evil-doing,
who urges that he is no guiltier than the rest, who
is not to be taught, not to be consoled, who will go
straight on in his path of evil. . . . The angry and
guilty man Lodovico symbolizes the absence of order
in Webster's universe" (pp. 34-35).

Despite the fact that what Leech says about the
character and course of action of Lodovico is sensible
enough, his conclusion that Lodovico "symbolizes the absence of order in Webster's universe" seems to me incorrect and misleading. See 16 below for a further note on
this.

[15] The Modern Theme, trans. James Cleugh (New York,
1933), p. 62.

[16] In the satires of Marston and his followers in
the same mode, the Malcontent figure has the role of truth-
speaker and the important function of unmasking the liars
and hypocrites around him. Despite Travis Bogard and a
majority of Webster's critics, I believe R. W. Dent to be
correct in his assertion that

"Flamineo is of all men the most deceived, the least

objective, in really essential matters, and that much
of his cynicism is but an inverted species of cant.
His vision has at best the clarity of an Iago, Edmund,
or Goneril, of all those who believe 'the text is foolish.' He knows neither himself, his fellows, nor the
world. And his 'wisdom' is refuted by the play. . . .

". . . Thus we can view such fruits of Webster's
borrowing . . . in two ways. If, like many critics, we
regard Flamineo as choric, we get artistic chaos. The
action of the play has stemmed from the conscious defiance of morality by the central trio. Like Lodovico's
outbursts in the initial scene, their evasions of re-
sponsibility should not be interpreted as Webster's.
Flamineo moved from the first with a thoroughly per-
verted system of values, complicated by an inability
he did not recognize to practice the politic art he
so admired. . . . In short, I prefer regarding Webster
as an effective dramatist who intentionally made muddled characters, rather than as a dramatist whose own
view of action was incredibly muddled" (pp. 28-31).

[17]G. K. Hunter makes this point about the Malcontent in Marston's drama (p. 101).

[18]Even Clifford Leech argues that Flamineo is to
be understood as a choral voice, a spokesman for the playwright (pp. 49-50).

[19]Leech, p. 52.

[20]The Guernica seems to me to render quite success-
fully in its own medium the same tragic paradox that in-
forms The White Devil. The figure of the man-beast amid
the carnage of the ruined city symbolizes the will to power;
having had its own way, it stands enigmatically among the
chaos of its own making.

[21]Elder Olson, in Tragedy and the Theory of Drama
(Detroit, 1961), suggests that the spectator in the theater learns what he learns about character through a series
of inferences he makes as the drama unfolds (see pp. 55-
85). This seems to me analogous to my point here.

[22]Her account of the dream in which she is set
upon in a graveyard by her husband and Brachiano's Duchess
(I, ii, 221-45) has puzzled several commentators. If we
see the ambiguity as to whether she is instructing her
lover in murder as a deliberate device to keep her character enigmatic the difficulty disappears. Webster uses
a similar device when he has the brutal murders of Camillo
and Isabella take place offstage, showing them in dumb
show with Brachiano watching. I suspect this last, however, to be also a question of aesthetic distancing.

[23]Jacobean Tragedy: The Quest for Moral Order
(London, 1962), pp. 97-122. His method allows him largely
to ignore the problems of plot and characterization that
have given Webster's other critics such pause.

[24]For a discussion of this view of character, see

J. L. Styan, The Elements of Drama (Cambridge, 1960),
pp. 163-87.

[25]Boklund, pp. 107-09. Professor Boklund argues
that there is little documentary evidence to support the
theory that Webster changed an innocent young husband into
the Camillo of the play. But if there is no evidence for
innocence and youth, there is none for the stock comic
figure of an old cuckold either.

[26]Machiavelli's concept of Fortune is discussed
by nearly every commentator on his theory. For a good
summary which emphasizes the mythopeic aspect of
Machiavelli's Fortune, see Albert William Levi, Literature,
Philosophy and the Imagination (Bloomington, 1962), Chapter
7, "Destiny, Fortune & Fate," pp. 229-72; see pp. 237-39
in particular.

[27]The link between images of disease, doctors, and
the body politic trope has been discussed at length, making
it difficult to add anything new. Webster uses so many
of them, however, that an attempt to evaluate the particulars of his usage may be in order; In the theory of the
time, disease results when the bodily fluids get out of
balance; an excess of blood, for instance, results in some
form of intemperance. This may be manifested in lust,
anger, pride, etc., all of which are related. (Thus when
Brachiano's lust is frustrated only "blood" will allay his
passion.) The function of the doctor is to restore harmony,

or better still, prevent the imbalance from occurring at all. By analogy, the function of right rule was to maintain harmony in the body politic. Lacking the knowledge that sickness may be caused by an outside agency, Webster and his contemporaries were quite naturally disturbed by the implications involved.

In Webster, doctors, like lawyers, are without exception, evil. It is taken as a matter of course that they grow rich on disease, are willing to poison for a fee, and where they do not kill they corrupt. The utopian mode of inculcating virtue in the young prince was to teach the ideal of law by means of maxim and right example. The habit of virtue thus built up in the prince would assure the health of the body politic. Machiavelli's factual approach, on the contrary, emphasized not what you should do but what you could do--strong and dangerous medicine for the weak, and by analogy, so too the factual approach to the study of medicine. The profession of law may also suffer such an ethical dislocation. Stripped of an informing ideal and visualized in a purely utilitarian light, such knowledge must have seemed diabolical indeed to the utopian moralist.

[28]Webster is extraordinarily adept at creating simultaneous perspectives. The effect is to externalize everything and, at the same time, provide the spectator with the aesthetic distance he needs to allow him to make ethical judgment.

What Webster is attempting, I think, is to circum-
vent the central dramatic problem of this type of tragedy,
how to combine a passionate and reckless will and self-
conscious guile. As I have suggested above, his method
consists largely of realizing these imperatives via several
characters. Thus what Arthur Sewell has to say about the
relationship of character and vision in Shakespeare would
apply even more to Webster: ". . . the essential process
of character-creation is a prismatic breaking-up of the
comprehensive vision of the play; and each element of
vision, so separated out, is in itself a unique illumina-
tion, finding its individual fulfilment in character"
(pp. 19-20).

On the importance of aesthetic distance in drama,
see Susanne Langer, "The Dramatic Illusion," pp. 306-25, in
Feeling and Form (New York, 1955)--pp. 318-20 in particular.
[29] The Individual and the Cosmos in Renaissance
Philosophy, trans. Mario Domandi (New York, 1964), pp. 76-77.
[30] Leonard Dean argues that Webster needs to be ap-
proached "with the right expectations. If one looks for
a straight-line plot or for realistic motivation, he will
be disappointed. The play [The Duchess of Malfi] is built
on different principles. The structure is that of analogous contrasting scenes which are essentially repetitive
and symbolic rather than progressive and symbolic."
Elizabethan Drama (New York, 1950), p. 22.

[31] I owe my ideas here about the importance of rebirth to the political to Hannah Arendt's The Human Condition (Garden City, 1958) and to Virgil's Aeneid.

I would suggest also that the powerful sense of
social continuity we feel at the close of Shakespeare's
Hamlet and Macbeth, say, is by no means characteristic of
all tragedy, not even all Shakespearean tragedy. About
the ending of Lear, D. G. James asserts, and I would agree:
". . . the ending of the play is not . . . an end which
looks on to a succeeding order and condition. . . .
The play at its end at most looks dimly ahead beyond
itself as, at its beginning, it had not looked back
to what had gone before. Shakespeare does not choose
to set it in an imagined history; it is more like a
fable which is told or an image which occurs and fades.
Its final note is anticipated death, and not renewed
and continuing life." The Dream of Learning (Oxford,
1951), p. 104. I cite this at length because it seems to
me to clarify an essential distinction between the moral
and the aesthetic. For a recent and very perceptive treatment of the aesthetic of tragedy, see Levi, pp. 308-14.

[32] The function of Flamineo's malcontent pose here
is the same as in III, i. It is, on one level, the conventional one. Behind his mask of mirth he can rail against
the conditions of the time, and again it is to the question of reward that he returns compulsively. The signif-

icant difference between him and his prototype, however,
is Flamineo's superiority to his role. His primary purpose is not so much to expose the evils of the time as
to hide himself behind the mask. It is to Marcello whom
he speaks here, and it is significant that the best Marcello
can do in his own defense is mouth platitudes about honesty
and virtue being their own reward. What Flamineo knows,
and Webster fears, is that where personal virtue is simply
another mask assumed for practical purposes, the genuine
article has but questionable value.

[33]See Ribner, for instance, for an interpretation
based upon such a Christian reading of Webster's imagery.

[34]The "success" of Monticelso is something of an
exception, and this is perhaps Webster's reason for allow-
ing him to disappear, so to speak, into his role after
he is elected Pope. On the other hand, to be frozen into
such a role is perhaps not to be seen as success either.
Leech sees the significance of Monticelso in primarily religious terms. While I cannot agree, I do find his analysis
suggestive:

". . . Monticelso in his more arid way seems to belong
with Isabella and Geovanni to the company of the good.
His election as Pope is not an irrelevancy, put in to
leave fascinated though Protestant England open-mouthed.
It is a suggestion that man, not altogether in vain,
strives to bring order into his affairs. Lodovico,

whose cry 'Banisht!' is the first word in the play,
and Brachiano, with his 'Quite Lost,' are outside the
scope of ordered life.

"There is a Calvanist strain in Jacobean drama
which is commonly overlooked. The tragic writers know
little of heaven but much of hell. Webster discrimi-
nates clearly between good and evil and, though his
characters refer much to the corruptive power of great
place, he does not condemn society outright. It is
woefully imperfect, but a Cardinal or Pope may do his
best to denounce guilt and to discourage revenge.
Courts may err and judges grow angry and accuse, but
laws may be just and justly exercised. And yet all
this seems irrelevant in the face of death and the consciousness of damnation. What comes after life may be
uncertain, but there is a terrible certainty in the
recognition of evil. That is the portion of Vittoria
and Flamineo, and their power to stare it in the face
gives them something of nobility. And that is worth
ambition, though in hell" (pp. 56-57).

[35] See Leonard F. Dean, "Richard II: The State and
the Image of the Theater," PMLA, Vol. 67, 1952, pp. 211-18.

[36] Leech, p. 55, mentions this fact in passing.

[37] For an interesting discussion of the court trial
as drama, see Harold Rosenberg, The Tradition of the New
(New York, 1959), pp. 163-65.

[38]The use of force is a sign that the obedience implicit in a hierarchical society has broken down.

[39]P. 43.

[40]Webster's most recent editor, John Russell Brown, in his Introduction to the Revels edition of The White Devil (London, 1960), suggests there is still some doubt about Webster's sole authorship and the date of Appius and Virginia (pp. xxv-xxvi). He seems to me to offer little more than Lucas, however, and there is nothing in Lucas (see below, Chapter IV) to contradict my view of the chronology of Webster's three tragedies.

CHAPTER III

THE DUCHESS OF MALFI

As I have attempted to show, the single most
important determinant in the world of The White Devil is
power. I have been describing this primarily in terms of
Machiavelli's theory, a system that attempts to assimilate
the conventions of men to the regularities of nature,

> . . . to see politics as a science where the law of
> causality holds, and where there is inherent necessity
> in political events as there is in the series of
> natural change.[1]

The advantages to the tragedian for the creation of the
dramatically essential illusion of inevitability are plain
enough. But there are certain inherent problems also, as
I noted in my discussion of the final scenes of the play.
In The Duchess of Malfi, written only a short time later,[2]
these problems have become more obvious, yet paradoxically,
Webster's none-too-successful attempt to recognize and
resolve them results, in my opinion, in a more profound
work of art.

If we view this second play not as a sequel, but
as a separate work which nevertheless embodies essentially
the same political-moral dialectic as the first, a view
that the plays themselves do much to encourage, some

interesting things emerge. To begin with, the all-
determining power relationship is negated in this play.
Not at once of course, but as the story unfolds. And
precisely at the center of Webster's "meaning" here is
this: human behavior, even in the Machiavellian court,
defies the rigid and sterile categorical imperatives of
Machiavelli's modes and orders. This breaking down of
the Machiavellian myth is the result of a process begun
in The White Devil. When Webster begins to look at his
Machiavellian characters as other than stereotypes, he
must allow them some status as human beings. What follows
from this is a modification of the Machiavellian stereotype
in the direction of a greater moral complexity. He comes
not so much to accept political immorality; he comes,
rather, to accept certain inevitabilities as part of a
secular politics.[3]

In dramatic terms, the two plays differ rather
radically in plot, character, and in the total impression
created by the imagery. In The White Devil, plot is the
dominant element, chiefly I believe because power relationships are the overriding realities. Such a structure of
events is possible, however, because the point of view
Webster maintains is consistently that of the characters
who conceive the world in these terms. Thus plot and
character function together to create a play which may be
described as classic in shape. The imagery, also, depicts

the world in highly artificial terms, terms no less real
despite this artificiality.

In The Duchess of Malfi, however, the center is
shifted. This play, like Hamlet, marks both the culmina-
tion and the end of a particular tragic convention, making
it difficult to see where the tragedy of Italianate murder
and intrigue might go from here. Interestingly enough,
the shift in Webster, like that in the older revenge convention that begins with The Spanish Tragedy and ends with
Hamlet,[4] also moves from plot to character, so to speak;
a movement which inevitably includes a corollary growth
in moral complexity. The first of Webster's tragedies
depicts its characters inevitably broken on the rack of
necessity--hence the classical feel of that play. The
second is consistently character-centered, and the plot
often suffers accordingly.

As I noted in connection with The White Devil,
the figure of Isabella (and her fate) prefigures the
Duchess-heroine of this play. We might note also that
Vittoria, especially in her trial scene, offers a direct
parody of the heroine of this play. I say parody because
in this play the natural impulse asserted by the heroine
against the static and unproductive world of Machiavellian
power ultimately proves not to be a deception, a white
devil. The Duchess proves, unlike Vittoria, to be as
pure as she is vital, and if Vittoria's final gesture seems

more fearless than hers, this is perhaps an inevitable
consequence of the latter's more prolonged agony and the
narrower margin of aesthetic distance between her and the
audience.

In the earlier play the central characters are
themselves evil as well as mistaken. Those who oppose and
finally murder Brachiano and his closest associates are
not seen to be morally good, despite the fact that they do
operate within a kind of ethic, albeit a brutal and primitive one. In The Duchess of Malfi, the Duchess herself is
good but appearances are against her. The evil in this
play is located in those who are most careful of appearances. The central problem, however, remains what it was
for the former play: how to determine true value in a
world where moral confusion is the norm.

This question is kept before us from the opening
speech of the play, Antonio's set piece about the moral
anarchy that results when the court, the fountainhead of
moral authority, becomes poisoned by "flattering Sicophants."
This relatively simplistic Christian view is only a point
of departure, however, in a play where the world of the
Italianate court is depicted as the only reality. Webster's
world in The Duchess of Malfi, therefore, is like that in
The White Devil, a world of secular politics that is the
context for a dialectic concerned with these questions:
May virtue in the conventional sense exist at all in the

court? And if so, How may it survive in such hostile sur-
roundings? And of paramount importance to the public weal,
How may true virtue be recognized where appearance is the
order of the day and survival itself may well depend on
maintaining a false appearance? As this dialectic emerges in
The Duchess of Malfi it polarizes around the opposition between the natural and the unnatural, the fruitful and the
sterile, the impulse and the calculated response--and
despite the Machiavellian frame and setting, the final
result for this play is the shattering of the myth. For
Webster, the political question--who governs?--is the
crucial one, subsuming as it does the ideological question--
by what symbols and myths?; the ethical question--who
benefits?; and the religious question--what is the quality
of life?

2

What Clifford Leech views as a decline in Webster's
dramatic skill between The White Devil and The Duchess of
Malfi should more properly be understood as the inevitable
consequence of a shift in focus between the two plays--
from the public world of action of the earlier to the
private world of this one, from the executioners to the
victims so to speak.[5] Leech's view, is, it seems to me,
a consequence of his understanding of Elizabethan tragedy,
up to and including Shakespeare's. His argument reveals

some interesting things about Webster's plays, but he is
led finally to the conclusion that the playwright's inconsistencies of characterization and ambiguities of plotting
indicate a confusion of intention that seriously affects
his dramaturgy.[6] Witness the following about The Duchess:

> This play works upon the nerves of the audience
> more skilfully than perhaps any other Jacobean
> tragedy. Outside the major works of Shakespeare (and
> perhaps even this customary exception is more unneces-
> sary), the death of the Duchess moves us more deeply
> than anything else in English drama. For its "great
> moments," indeed, this play may stand higher than The
> White Devil. Yet we may come to the conclusion that,
> for all its occasional splendours, The Duchess of
> Malfi gives fair warning of Webster's imminent decline
> in dramatic power. He has excelled in the moving
> exploration of the human mind, yet his play is blurred
> in its total meaning. It is a collection of brilliant
> scenes, where statements do not ultimately cohere.[7]

The same could be said of Hamlet--and it would be both
right and wrong about that play also, if Shakespeare had
written no more tragedy after Hamlet, or had written only
an Appius and Virginia. To be logically consistent Leech
would have to conclude that The Spanish Tragedy is a
greater play than Hamlet because of its relatively greater

clarity. Later in his book, he argues something very close to such a conclusion:

> Yet it remains true that the plays of the sixteenth century are, in general, illustrations of a set thesis. We are not only clear what the plays are about, we are fairly sure of the kind of attitude the dramatist wishes us to take. But in Jacobean years this clarity and this certainty largely evaporate.[8]

Again, one can agree with everything but the implied conclusion--that the lack of a set thesis must lead to a decline in dramatic power. As a matter of fact, in the case of Appius and Virginia the reverse is true: the loss of dramatic power is a direct consequence of Webster's having a set thesis.

To be fair with Leech, however, it is necessary to quote him once more in connection with the change in the drama that takes place as Elizabethan moves into Jacobean:

> When we consider the relation of Jacobean tragedy to the twentieth century stage, we are always--and rightly--inclined to emphasize its rhetoric, its greater range of style, its lack of inhibition. But in Jacobean eyes the playhouse was achieving a new naturalism, an acting-style which was appropriate to the new drama of infirm orientation, the drama that explored and documented [italics mine] but was no straightforward illustration of a given thesis.[9]

W. B. Yeats' distinction between poetry and rhetoric is
apposite here: rhetoric, he said, was the argument he
had with others, poetry the argument he had with himself.
Now, if it were possible to make the value judgment Leech
implies, that rhetoric makes for greater drama, we would
be stuck with its corollary, that poetry is, dramatically
speaking, destructive. That Leech would also reject such
a distinction is implied in such phrases as the italicized
above.

  If we see this matter as a question of degree,
however, Yeats' distinction contains a valuable insight.
Webster's argument with himself begins in The White Devil,
but it seldom gets out of hand in that play. His control
derives in part from the fact that there is something oversimple in the image of the human predicament as it is depicted in this play. He seems satisfied for the most part
to let his historically received material guide his hand.
(By historically received material, I mean both the conventions of the Machiavellian plot and the moral conflict
of the heroic characters.) To put the matter differently,
Webster accepts and makes brilliant use of an already
existing myth in this, the first of his tragedies. The
Duchess of Malfi is another matter altogether. Webster's
argument with himself has grown more intense in this play,
and the play's greater poetic power is a consequence of
this increase in intensity.

The public world of <u>The Duchess</u> is very similar
to the public world of <u>The White Devil</u>, but the playwright
is now chiefly concerned with an image left in the background in the earlier play, the image of private virtue
as victim in the world of the Italianate court. Just as
Hamlet found Denmark to be a prison, so too the Duchess
finds her world. Hamlet, however, knows from the start
what the audience comes to understand only gradually; the
Duchess, on the other hand, and the audience are at one
from the start, and we must participate with her in her
discovery.

When the play opens the central fact of life for
the young widow is imprisonment. In her case the difficulty is compounded by the fact that she is a ruler, but
one powerless to remake her court in her own image. She
is powerless to change the political reality which imprisons
her, and how much of her attraction to Antonio and the
essentially private joys of love and family is a consequence
of political frustration is left problematic. No one,
however, has ever found her love for Antonio to be lacking
in believability. Antonio is presented as a thoroughly
worthy man in everything but birth, and if Webster is to
avoid even the suggestion of unworthy motive on his part,
he must make him circumspect and retiring as lover-husband
to his rich prize.

Paradoxically, the Duchess' attempt to escape into simple personal concerns serves only to entrap her the more completely. With the birth of her children and her consequent loss of reputation she becomes even more vulnerable. Her rank is used against her by her politically astute and ruthless brothers, and, much more serious in its ultimate consequences, her love for husband and children is used to hold and to torture her. The imperatives of the Machiavellian court operate here just as they do in The White Devil, and the Machiavellian choices are approximately the same: to live in a climate where success, even survival, requires the suppression of natural instinct, or to give up one's place in the public world entirely, choosing instead to live and die in private obscurity away from the court.[10] But in asserting the claims of natural impulse in the person of the Duchess and the situation of her love and secret marriage, Webster creates another human imperative; and in this play the natural impulse is not merely swept aside and destroyed as it is in The White Devil.

It is to create this image of naturalness and innocence that Webster employs the "Ovidian" imagery which seems so out of place in his Italianate court. Examples of such imagery may be found throughout the play; but to cite only the most obvious instance, witness the love scene between the Duchess and Antonio:

DUCH. I'll stop your mouth   [kisses him.]

ANT. Nay, that's but one, Venus had two soft Doves
To draw her Chariot: I must have another: [kisses her.]
When wilt thou marry, Cariola?

CAR. Never (my Lord.)

ANT. O fie upon this single life: forgoe it:
We read how Daphne, for her peevish flight
Became a fruitlesse Bay-tree: Sirinx turn'd
To the pale empty Reede: Anaxarete
Was frozen into Marble: whereas thos
Which married, or prov'd kind unto their friends
Were, by a gracious influence, transhap'd
Into the Oliffe, Pomgranet, Mulbery:
Became Flowres, precious Stones, or eminent Starres.

CAR. This is vaine Poetry: but I pray you tell me,
If there were propos'd me, Wisdome, Riches, and Beauty,
In three severall young men, which should I choose?

ANT. 'Tis a hard question: This was Paris' case
And he was blind in't, and there was great cause:
For how was't possible he could judge right,
Having three amorous Goddesses in view,
And they starcke naked? 'twas a Motion
Were able to be-night the apprehention
Of the seveerest Counsellor of Europe.
Now I look on both your faces, so well form'd,
It puts me in mind of a question, I would aske.

CAR. What is't?

ANT. I doe wonder why hard-favour'd Ladies
For the most part, keepe worse-favour'd waieting women,
To attend them, and cannot endure faire-ones.
    DUCH. Oh, that's soone answer'd.
Did you ever in your life know an ill Painter
Desire to have his dwelling next doore to the shop
Of an excellent Picture-maker? 'twould disgrace
His face-making, and undoe him: I pre-thee
When were we so merry? my haire tangles.

                              (III, ii, 26-61)

The "golden world" figured in passages such as the above
is significant beyond the particular scene, as I have suggested. Witness the parody of this scene provided in the
Cardinal-Julia exchange in II, iv, for instance, where
love is lust and the gold proves false and deceptive. In
contrast to the Duchess, Julia is described in terms of
the caged bird freed:

    CARD. You may thanke me, (Lady)
I have taken you off your mellancholly pearch,
Boare you upon my fist, and shew'd you game,
And let you flie at it: I pray thee kisse me--
When thou wast with thy husband, thou wast watch'd
Like a tame Ellephant: (still you are to thanke me)
Thou hadst onely kisses from him, and high feeding,
But what delight was that? 'twas just like one

That hath a little fingring on the Lute,

Yet cannot tune it: (still you are to thanke me.)

                      (II, iv, 38-48)

She is to pay dearly for her freedom. The Cardinal proves
not only a cold lover but a harsh master. Julia's error is
instructive, however, since it is a false conception of
pleasure that leads her into the Cardinal's clutches.

This problem of how to tell true pleasure from
false in a deceptive world of appearances is important
here. It is, moreover, a major theme of Webster's
explicitly political elegy written on the occasion of the
death of Henry, the young Prince of Wales.[11] The elegy is
conventional in the sentiment expressed, and but for the
fact that the imagery is so strikingly like that of the
tragedies, especially The Duchess, one might well leave it
out of consideration here. I find especially interesting
the passage (lines 152-98) which tells the story of how
Jupiter sent Pleasure into the world for the benefit of
mortals and how, delighted with her reception, she forgot
her former home in heaven and the god who had sent her.
Jupiter, angered at the slight, recalled her in thunder,
at which she spread her wings and flew back. She left
behind her robe, however, lest it contaminate heaven with
mortal taint. At this, Sorrow, who had been living in
exile in the galleys as punishment for having corrupted
the court, came crawling back, hoping to be reinstated

at court. She had no luck, however, till by chance she
found Pleasure's discarded robe. She took it up, painted
her face to the current fashion, and shortly came to rule
in the place previously occupied by the true Pleasure.
The result was of course devastating, for mortals flocked
to follow her.

> . . . straight from <u>Country</u>, <u>Citty</u>, and from <u>Court</u>,
> Both without wit or number there resort
> Many to this imposter--all adore
> Her haggish false-hood, <u>Usurers</u> from their store
> Supply her and are cosened, <u>Citizens</u> buy
> Her forged titles, riot and ruine flye,
> Spreading their poison universally.
> Nor are the bosomes of great <u>Statesmen</u> free
> From her intelligence, who let's them see
> Themselves and fortunes in false perspectives;
> Some landed Heires consort her with their wives,
> Who being a baud corrupts their all-spent oathes--
> They have entertain'd the divill in <u>Pleasures</u> cloaths.
> And since this cursed maske, which to our cost
> Lasts day and night, we have entirely lost
> <u>Pleasure</u>, who from heaven wils us be advis'd,
> That our false <u>Pleasure</u> is but <u>Care</u> disguis'd.
>
>   (176-92)

To Lucas, this is

one of Webster's characteristic parables; and characteristically inapposite, for after all, the hollowness
of worldly pleasures has very little to do with the
failure of hopes so justly attached to Prince Henry's
youthful promise.[12]

But Lucas is mistaken, for in Webster's way of
looking, there is a close connection between the two.
Natural impulse, a sense of animal vitality, the life force
if you will, continues to exert itself in the world of men
with or without the moral exemplar envisioned in the person
of Prince Henry. Without proper moral guidance, men follow a false image, Sorrow disguised as Pleasure. The concluding lines of the poem reinforce such a reading and,
furthermore, link up the concept of the moral exemplar with
the importance of fame and reputation and the function of
the poet:

Yet though his praise heere beare so short a wing,
Thames hath more Swannes, that will his praises sing
In sweeter tunes, bee-pluming his sad Horace,
And his three fethers, while men live, or verse.
And by these signes of love let great men know,
That sweete and generous favour they bestow
Upon the Muses, never can be lost:

For they shall live by them, when all the cost

Of guilded Monuments shall fall to dust;

"They grave in metle that sustaines no rust.

"Their wood yeelds hony and industrious Bees,

"Kills Spiders, and their webs, like Irish Trees.

"A Poets pen like a bright Scepter swaies

"And keepes in awe dead mens dispraise or praise.

Thus tooke He acquittance of all worldly strife,

"The evening showes the day, and death crownes life.

(313-28)

Twelve years later, in his masque, Monuments of Honor,[13]
Webster shows a continuing concern for these same themes.
In the final passages, worthy prince Henry's fame is de-
scribed as a phoenix that will live forever.

Characteristically, Webster judges value by its
effect in the world of men, and in this respect he is also
interested in the reputation a man leaves behind at his
death. And thus the poet's function, to record and perhaps even improve upon the image of the prince, for in
the absence of a divinely ordained authority, it is
necessary to extol the human, focusing upon both the real
and possible glory in man, so that a secular politics may
have some image of excellence to base itself in. Seen from
this perspective, we can better understand the intensity
of such "out of character"[14] speeches as the following,
where Bosola, having discovered the identity of the Duchess'

husband, appears to rejoice in a vision of political
re-birth. (We might look at the speeches immediately pre-
ceding this passage also, for it is Webster's irony that
the feigned disgrace of Antonio should be the occasion
that trips up the Duchess.)

> BOS. . . . these [courtiers] are Rogues; that in's
> prosperitie,
> But to have waited on his [Antonio's] fortune, could
> have wish'd
> His durty Stirrop rivited through their noses:
> And follow'd after's Mule, like a Beare in a Ring.
> Would have prostituted their daughters, to his Lust:
> Made their first-borne Intelligencers: thought none
> happy
> But such as were borne under his bless'd Plannet
> And wore his Livory: and doe these Lyce drop off now?
> Well, never looke to have the like againe;
> He hath left a sort of flattring rogues behind him,
> Their doombe must follow: Princes pay flatterers,
> In their owne money: Flatterers dissemble their vices,
> And they dissemble their lies, that's Justice:
> Alas, poore gentleman!--
> DUCH. Poore! he hath amply fill'd his cofers.
> BOS. Sure he was too honest: Pluto the god of
> riches,
> When he's sent (by Jupiter) to any man

He goes limping, to signifie that wealth

That comes on god's name, comes slowly, but when he's

                    sent

On the divells arrand, he rides poast, and comes in

                    by scuttles:

Let me shew you, what a most unvalu'd jewell,

You have (in a wanton humour) throwne away,

To blesse the man shall find him: He was an excellent

Courtier, and most faithfull, a souldier, that thought

                    it

As beastly to know his owne value too little,

As devillish to acknowledge it too much,

Both his vertue, and forme, deserv'd a farre better

                    fortune:

His discourse rather delighted to judge it selfe, then

                    shew it selfe.

His breast was fill'd with all prefection,

And yet it seem'd a private whispring roome.

It made so little noyse of't.

    DUCH. But he was basely descended.

    BOS. Will you make your selfe a mercinary herald,

Rather to examine mens pedegrees, then vertues?

You shall want him.

For know an honest states-man to a Prince,

Is like a Cedar, planted by a Spring,

The Spring bathes the trees roote, the gratefull tree

Rewards it with his shadow: you have not done so--
I would sooner swim to the <u>Bermoothes</u> on
Two Politisians' rotten bladders, tide
Together with an Intelligencers hart-string
Then depend on so changeable a Princes favour.
Fare-thee-well (<u>Antonio</u>) since the mallice of the world
Would needes downe with thee, it cannot be sayd yet
That any ill happened unto thee,
Considering thy fall was accompanied with vertue.

    DUCH. Oh, you render me excellent Musicke.

    BOS. Say you?

    DUCH. This good one that you speake of, is my
                                 husband.

    BOS. Do I not dreame? can this ambitious age
Have so much goodnes in't, as to prefer
A man, meerely for worth: without these shadowes
Of wealth and painted honors? possible?

    DUCH. I have had three children by him.

    BOS. Fortunate Lady,
For you have made your private nuptiall bed
The humble, and faire Seminary of peace,
No question but: many an unbenific'd Scholler
Shall pray for you, for this deed, and rejoyce
That some preferment in the world can yet
Arise from merit. The virgins of your land
(That have no dowries) shall hope your example

Will raise them to rich husbands: Should you want

Souldiers 'twould make the very Turkes and Moores

Turne Christians, and serve you for this act.

Last, the neglected Poets of your time,

In honour of this trophee of a man,

Rais'd by that curious engine, (your white hand)

Shall thanke you, in your grave, for't; and make that

More reverend then all the Cabinets

Of living Princes: for Antonio

His fame shall likewise flow from many a pen,

When Heralds shall want coates, to sell to men.

       (III, ii, 268-341)

   The above seventy-odd lines presents in contrasting
images Webster's obsessive theme: the failure of Justice,
where the court, the spring and fountainhead, is corrupted.
In terms of plot and action, this same scene begins the
Duchess' fateful decline into public scandal. She rashly
chooses to leave her refuge and attempt to escape to
Ancona by way of the Shrine at Loretto,where the Cardinal,
ever conscious of appearance, is shortly to divest himself
ritually of the role of churchman and don that of soldier.
Both this and the following scene in which the Duchess,
with her family and those who remain of her followers, is
refused sanctuary at Loretto, are enacted in dumb show.
The effect is to speed up the action and to make it

symbolic. Thus Act III, scene ii, stands at a point in the
action where an emblematic summary is quite in order; moreover, in giving this speech to Bosola, Webster both
complicates Bosola's already complex perspective and pre-
pares for his "reform" after the death of the Duchess.[15]

But to return for a moment to the question of
justice and the perspective offered at this important
juncture in the action. What happens to the Duchess in
the following scenes, up to and including her death, symbolizes the fate of the natural and virtuous in a state
without justice. The function of the mad-men is primarily
to universalize Webster's meaning, and the whole atmosphere
of Act IV emphasizes the remoteness of a possible rebirth
in a world where individual will has become its own law.
Act V, therefore, does not so much deal out poetic justice
to the cruel and calculating Cardinal and his mad brother,
Duke Ferdinand; rather, it presents the tragic implications
of power without an informing vision.[16] If you divorce
public performance from private virtue you may indeed
succeed; the price in humanity, however, may be terrifying
to contemplate.

The Arrgonian brothers, like Othello, learn too
late they have thrown away a priceless gem in destroying
their sister. Their successes turn to ashes; the penalty,
a total meaninglessness. Instead of the sweetness of
revenge, there is only the dreadful fatigue of,

Cover her face: Mine eyes dazell: she di'd yong.

(IV, ii, 281)

We see that there is considerably more to the closing up of
the tragic structure than the death of the protagonist,
especially in this play, where the entire last act is
devoted to denoument. As Richard Sewall writes in his
essay on the tragic form:

> . . . the perception which completes the tragic form
> is not dramatized solely through the hero's change,
> although his pilgrimage provides the traditional tragic
> structure. The full nature and extent of the new vision
> is measured also by what happens to the other figures
> in the total symbolic situation--to the hero's
> antagonists (King Creon, Cladius, Iago); to his
> opposites (the trimmers and hangers-on, the Osrics); to
> his approximates (Ismene, Horatio, Kent, the Chorus).
> Some he moves, some do not change at all. But his
> suffering must make a difference somewhere outside
> himself. . . .[17]

For Bosola, the important point-of-view character, the
virtue of the Duchess provided a startling revelation of
the possibility of virtue in the court; her courage in
the face of torture and death confirms this, and the sight
of her dead works a curious reformation in him. Not a
change, but a discovery of what has been there in him all

along:

> Oh, she's gone againe: there the cords of life breake:
>
> Oh sacred Innocence, that sweetly sleepes
>
> On Turtles feathers: whil'st a guilty conscience
>
> Is a blacke Register, wherein is writ
>
> All our good deedes, and bad: A Perspective
>
> That showes us hell; that we cannot be suffer'd
>
> To doe good when we have a mind to it!
>
> . . .
>
> (IV, ii, 382-88)

What happens in the final act is at most but nega-
tively affirmative, suggesting the consequences in human
terms of anarchic willfulness. The image of the Duchess
remains, however, if only as an echo from the grave, transformed by her death into a symbol of human possibility in
this worst of all possible worlds.

Just as in The White Devil, Webster offers no way
out in this play either, for he can show no way of making
this image politically viable in any significant way.
He has succeeded, however, in penetrating through the
Machiavellian myth to a more significant and truer vision
of human reality--his Machiavels either discover their
own humanity and reform, or become the victims of their
own miscalculation about themselves and the world.
Humanized, the Machiavel becomes, ironically, his own
victim.

Instead of a detailed analysis of how each character meets his death and what this means in terms of Webster's
tragic vision,[18] I would like to keep the emphasis of this
essay upon the political implications of what happens in
Act V, and how this links up with the death of Webster's
heroine. Despite the impressiveness of arguments such
as Ellis-Fermor's, I am not at all convinced that Webster's
tragic point is "the progress of the minds of the central
figures towards deeper and deeper self-knowledge. . .",
as she contends. I do not wish to argue that Webster's
tragedy is a type of epic drama in the sense that Brecht's
is, although Appius and Virginia might fruitfully be viewed
from that point of view; what I do wish to argue is that
to emphasize the progress of the individual soul towards
a confused and rather dubious insight into the nature of
reality--and this is more or less the conventional view,
from Lucas through Ellis-Fermor's excellent study, up to
and including Robert Ornstein's recent book--is to miss
an important, if not the important, point about Webster's
tragedy. Although Professor Ellis-Fermor is able to show
convincing evidence for such a growth in Bosola,[19] it is
difficult to accept her conclusion that there is an
important point in his discovery at the point of death that
life is confused and meaningless, "a mist." Whereas she
is correct in seeing as significant Webster's almost
compulsive re-examination of certain characters and motifs,

she is mistaken in her conclusion as to what this means.

In <u>The Duchess</u>, Webster's point may be brought
into relief, I feel, by contrasting the death of the
Duchess herself and that of Webster's most consummate
Machiavellian, the Cardinal. According to Ellis-Fermor,
"the true Machiavellian which Flamineo nearly was finds
consummation in the figure of the Cardinal."[20]

Nothing shakes him and nothing confuses him: his han-
dling of Bosola, who has discovered his complicity
in the Duchess's murder and has him in his power, is
so rapid, clear and ruthless that the lead comes again
into his own hands against all expectation. Though
he loses ground a little in the last act by the net
which he weaves for himself (the consummate Machiavellian should fall a victim to no man's machinations,
only to chance), he redeems himself at the last. He,
too, in respect of fortune, is but one of

> The Starres' tennys-halls (strooke and banded
> Which way please them),

but in respect of his own mind he is as secure a stoic
as the upright Delio and Antonio, having the courage
of his own ill-doing, as Appius after him, and redeem-
ing himself by it much as Appius does. His spirit,
burdened with the very deed that has driven Ferdinand
mad, gives no sign. "How tedious is a guilty conscience," he says; he is "puzzell'd in a question about

hell" and sees, in the clear water of the fish-pool,
"A thing, arm'd with a Rake." That is all. Never
does Webster tell us more of this character than when,
leaving him alone upon the stage in soliloquy, he tells
us only this. Such, as Webster discovers it to us,
is the Machiavellian reticence; at the end his brevity
stands compact against the loquacity of the dying
Ferdinand and Bosola and his last words, a suggestive
variant of Hamlet's, close a volume that we have never
been able to read except obliquely. He keeps his counsel to the end; we are never suffered a sight of the
workings of that impenetrable mind; death does not
move him from a life-time's reticence. When he can
no longer scheme, direct and control, he asks not for
pity, forgiveness or understanding, but to be "layd by,
and never thought of." He alone, of the Jacobean stage
Machiavellians, is worthy to stand beside the prototype of all politicians.[21]

Surely she is correct to see how fascinated Webster is by
the enigmatic politician. The burden of her discussion,
however, points elsewhere and, it seems to me, misses the
real significance of the place characters such as Francisco
and, in this play, the Cardinal, occupy. I would like to
suggest that Webster's point is the irony revealed by the
contrast between this "silent" life and death, and the very
different life and death of the Duchess. The consummate

politician, the man who concerned himself wholly with policy, to the point where he became perfect in it, revealing nothing of his true self even in death, recognizes (or does he?--what _is_ important for the irony here is that _we_ recognize) the absolute meaninglessness of his life and of his death. Ultimately he must remain a _what_, a kind of nothing. The Duchess, by contrast, is immensely meaningful in death, as she was in life. This is the real point of such final utterances as Delio's, a speech which Ellis-Fermor mistakenly cites as evidence that Webster's mind is divided, "pulled between two interpretations," which he attempted unsuccessfully to reconcile. In the following passage, the final speech of the play, Webster closes up his tragic form; and while it is true that he sees no way for virtue to survive in such a world, the fact remains that the concept expressed here is most important to his vision:

> These wretched eminent things
> Leave no more fame behind 'em, then should one
> Fall in a frost, and leave his print in snow--
> As soone as the sun shines, it ever melts,
> Both forme, and matter: I have ever thought
> Nature doth nothing so great, for great men,
> As when she's pleas'd to make them Lords of truth:

Integrity of life, is fame's best friend,

Which nobley (beyond Death) shall crowne the end.

(V, v, 138-46)

As we have seen, the Duchess was the least of politicians. Yet we know in her case both the what and the
who.[22] And it is this which makes her life and death
tragically meaningful. The tragic irony is that in the
world predicated by the play her death should have so
little meaning. That the Cardinal, whose whole life and
energy was given to political things, should leave not a
wrack behind at his death, is the real point here. But
the recognition is ours, and whether it is also the
Cardinal's, despite Professor Ellis-Fermor, is really
beside the point.

In Appius and Virginia Webster succeeds in transforming his heroine into a political artifact, but that
play is closer to what Frye would call secular auto[23] than
to tragedy. A consequence of Webster's steady movement
toward such a solution of his moral-political dilemma is
the progressively earlier deaths of his heroines: in The
White Devil Vittoria dies in the final scene of Act V; in
this play the Duchess dies in the final scene of Act IV;
and in Webster's last tragedy, Virginia dies in the first
scene of Act IV. The demands of Webster's political
moralism exert great pressure upon his tragic structures;

with The Duchess of Malfi he appears to have realized the precarious balance of great tragedy for the first and last time.

134

NOTES TO CHAPTER III

[1]Levi, p. 237.

[2]See Works, II, pp. 1-5, which dates the play after
The White Devil and before December of 1614.

[3]This shows most clearly in characters such as
Francisco de Medicis. Although the distinction between
politicians in The White Devil remains the rather crude
one of success and failure (despite the suggestiveness of
figures such as Isabella, who has a political conscience
in addition to a conventional morality), there is clearly
a distinction to be noted between the motives of Francisco
and the Cardinal on the one hand, and Brachiano and his
followers on the other. There is a kind of morality of
necessity in what Francisco does, though "reasons of state"
applied to individual persons seems brutal indeed. Moreover, Francisco is capable of such distinctions only up
to a certain point. His motive for revenge is a desire
for personal satisfaction, and the politically good man
is one who defines himself as part of the group rather
than seeing the whole in terms of his own ego.

[4]John Lawlor, The Tragic Sense in Shakespeare (New
York, 1960), argues convincingly that Hamlet's question-
ing of the imperative to avenge his father is a reflec-
tion of a growing Renaissance concern with a complex
ethical problem: Revenge or Justice? Once such a question is asked, he contends, the imperative to avenge loses

force, providing something less than the Necessity required by the tragic form. See in particular Chapter II,
"Agent or Patient?" pp. 45-73.

[5]This is not to say that the world of the play has
itself changed, since it is still recognizably the same
world. But a balance has been redressed in that we are
allowed to see the same world from a slightly different
perspective.

[6]Taken overall Leech's view seems to me a rather
more subtle variant of the Webster-as-decadent-Elizabethan
theory. But perhaps I do him an injustice--he is, it
seems to me, Webster's best critic. (See pp. 66-68 for
his catalog of Webster's confusions and inconsistencies,
and cf. Boklund, p. 67.)

[7]P. 65.

[8]P. 112.

[9]P. 63. Cf. E. H. Gombrich, Meditations on a Hobby
Horse, and Other Essays on the Theory of Art (London, 1963),
pp. 35-37. Gombrich argues that an artistically sophisticated audience makes increasingly greater demands upon
both artist and form, but also becomes more knowledgeable
about conventions and increasingly willing to meet the
artist half-way. What Leech describes as "drama of in-
firm orientation" may show these formal difficulties only
when compared to Elizabethan and/or modern drama.

[10]Witness Lear to Cordelia after he has come to

an understanding of who he is and what his real needs are:

"Come let's away

to prison:

We two alone will sing like birds i' the cage:

When thou dost ask me blessing, I'll kneel down,

And ask of thee forgiveness: so we'll live,

And pray, and sing, and tell old tales, and laugh,

At gilded butterflies, and hear poor rogues

Talk of court news; and we'll talk with them too,

Who loses and who wins; who's in, who's out;

And take upon's the mystery of things,

As if we were God's spies: and we'll wear out,

In a wall'd prison, packs and sects of great ones,

That ebb and flow by the moon."

(V, iii, 8-18)

[11]A Monumental Columne, registered Dec. 25, 1612. Works, III, 266-92.

[12]P. 289, Note to lines 152-98.

[13]Works, III, 311-39.

[14]This is characteristic of both The White Devil and this play; we need only recall Francisco's many out-of-character speeches in the former, especially toward the end of that play.

[15]Note that in III, ii, we are reminded that Bosola is a man of parts, a man with a history, who was a scholar at the university, etc., thus making him qualified to speak

with a broad knowledgeability. Like Flamineo, he abandoned
the contemplative life of observer to become the man of
action.

[16]Travis Bogard argues that Webster's vision is
both tragic and satiric:

"As Webster darkens the world of his tragedy, life
appears to become an increasing agony. What had been
aberration to the earlier satirists becomes to Webster
the norm. Each evil is a symbol of death, each abuse
a step toward it. In the end what his satire revealed
of the true nature of life is fused with the outcome
of his tragic story. The ultimate tragedy of Webster's
world is not the death of any individual but the presence of evil and decay which drags all mankind to death.
The function of the satire is to reveal man's common
mortality and his involvement in evil; the tragic story
is the story of a few who find courage to defy such
revelation. In their defiance there is a glory for
mankind, and in their struggle and assertion lies the
brilliance of Websterian tragedy" (p. 147).

I cannot agree, for such a view fails to take into
consideration the political fact of the reality of power
and the very real dilemma created by a situation not so
much immoral as morally confused.

[17]"The Tragic Form," Essays in Criticism, IV, No. 4,
357-58.

[18]I doubt that what I might have to say here would add significantly to what several other critics have already had to say on this subject. See in particular the excellent study of Clifford Leech already cited, and Una Ellis-Fermor's The Jacobean Drama, pp. 170-90.

[19]Her description of Bosola is particularly revealing I feel:

"Our interest in the figure of Bosola, for example, is not mainly because, in the service of Ferdinand's mania, he murders the Duchess and brings about unwittingly the death of Antonio, but because of the strange discrepancy between the man he appears, the man he would be and the man that, unknown to himself, he really is. Our interest is intense first because we are watching the slow permeation of his outer consciousness by this inner self, the slow summation of all his findings in the knowledge of himself . . ." p. 176.

[20]p. 179.

[21]p. 180.

[22]Before her death the Duchess achieved the calm of mind, the state of readiness that signals the moment just before death of the tragic protagonist. Richard Sewall describes it well:

". . . Having at first resented his destiny, he has lived it out, found unexpected meanings in it, carried his case to a more-than-human tribunal. He sees his

own destiny, and man's destiny, in its ultimate perspective" (p. 358).

[23]See *Anatomy of Criticism*, pp. 165-68, for a treatment of secular *auto* as a particular dramatic genre.

CHAPTER IV

APPIUS AND VIRGINIA

Webster's third and last tragedy was written more
than a decade after The Duchess of Malfi, in 1625-27, according to the estimate of Lucas.[1] Its chief virtues are
the relatively pallid ones of consistency and clarity.
In any case, the virtues of Appius and Virginia are not
those of his two earlier tragedies.[2] The vision of evil
is gone: here evil is defined and localized rather precisely. Also gone is the sense of inevitability, that this
is what must be I have been associating with Classical and
Shakespearean tragedy. In this play Webster appears to
have had things fully conceptualized from the start, and
its failure as tragedy is a consequence of this. Perhaps
the difficulty is latent in any vision of the human lot
which is primarily political--how, for instance, see
Virgil's Aeneas as tragic hero? Karl Jaspers states it
concisely:

> Tragic knowledge invades and breaks through, but does
> not master, reality--there is too much it leaves un-
> touched, forgotten, or unexplained. It lures us into
> an exalting realm of grandeur; and thus, despite all
> clear-eyed honesty, it obscures the truth. . . .
>
> Tragic knowledge thus has its limits: it achieves
> no comprehensive interpretation of the world. It fails

to master universal suffering; it fails to grasp the whole terror and insolubility in men's existence.[3]

Yet Appius and Virginia is not an epic, nor is it a species of comedy, despite the too thoroughly intellectualized feel of the play. The shape of tragedy is still here, but the sense of ambiguity attendant upon a tragic perception of man and the universe is missing. Searching for a comparison, one thinks of the Roman tragedies of Ben Jonson. But the comparison is not a good one, since Webster's play contains almost nothing satiric, and Jonson's, despite his ostensible intent, are realized in a satiric mode. The moral seriousness of this play reminds one somewhat of Shakespeare's Roman plays, or those of his histories which approach the tragic. Like the Roman plays, especially Julius Caesar, Appius and Virginia is characterized by an obvious philosophic dialectic; like the histories, the play embodies a secular mythos, one which Webster's contemporaries may have found deeply compelling. Unhappily, however, Webster's play, unlike Shakespeare's, fails to have significance beyond whatever point it may have had for its own time.

One possible reason for the neatness of this play, a quality especially remarkable when the play is compared with the two earlier tragedies, is the focus of interest, which appears not to be character but the configuration of the ideas. Precisely because of the play's weaknesses--

I am not at all convinced, however, that the absence of
a compelling interest in character is necessarily a weak-
ness[4]--it is relatively easy, I believe, to trace out the
pattern of Webster's thought here. The exercise is worth-
while because of the light it sheds on the two earlier
tragedies.

Webster's source, which itself was drawn from
legendary Roman tradition, was an obvious one in view of
his philosophic preconceptions. Lucas summarizes the
legend in his first footnote to scene i:

Decemviri: in 451 B.C. after long dissensions
between the patricians and plebians it was agreed
to appoint a board of Ten (Decemviri) to codify the
laws. They were given supreme power for their year
of office and used it so well that a similar board
was elected for a second year to complete their work.
The one Decemvir re-elected was Appius Claudius; who
now took advantage of his position to turn the Decem-
virate into a tyranny, till he was overthrown after
Virginia's death by a popular rising, in 449. . . .[5]

2

The opening scene of the play, which depicts the
attempt by certain city officials to recruit Appius for
a second term, suggests that Webster patterned it after

the scene in <u>Richard III</u> in which Richard pretends not
to want the crown. A reading of Webster's source shows,
however, that he probably took this directly from his
source.[6] Webster manages to keep the scene from both
comedy or melodrama by a series of minor reversals, and
about half-way through the scene Appius is virtually in-
vested in the ceremonial robes of high office. In fewer
than 150 lines, we learn much about the political configuration which is the basis of the action and, moreover,
about the nature of political reality as Webster seems
to have visualized it. We get this last mostly from Appius
himself, whose knowledge of the imperatives of office makes
clear why he is their obvious choice:

> . . . he that must steer at th' head of an Empire,
> ought to be the Mirrour of the times for Wisdome and
> for Policie. . . .
>
> (I, i, 14-16)

> I am given up
> To a long travell full of fear and danger,
> To waste the day in sweat, and the cold night
> In a most desolate contemplation,
> Banisht from all my kindred and my friends,
> Yea banisht from my selfe; for I accept
> This honourable calling.
>
> (I, i, 87-93)

                . . . this reverend seat

        Receives me as a pupill, rather gives

        Ornament to the person, then our person

        The least grace to it. . . .

        I am to travell; 'tis a certaine truth:

        Look by how much the labour of the minde

        Exceeds the bodie's, so far am I bound

        With paine and industry, beyond the toyle

        Of those that sweat it worre, beyond the toyle

        , Of any Artisan--pale cheeks, and sunk eyes,

        A head with watching dizied, and a haire

        Turn'd white in youth, all these at a dear rate

        We purchase speedily that tend a State.

                                (I, i, 120-32)

The second scene is set in the house of Virginius
(patrician-soldier and father to Virginia) and the juxta-
position of the private with the public place of Scene i
is important to Webster's meaning; how important it is
will become clear as the action unfolds. The action of
this scene has also a quality of ritual about it: Numitorius,
in the absence of his brother Virginius, is presiding over
the formal betrothal of Virginia to Icilius, a young
gentleman of the city who has recently been raised to
knighthood. Old Virginius is with his soldiers, several
hours distant from the city, where he is attempting to
keep down a mutiny, the result of Rome's failure to provision

their camp. The tone of the scene is formal, almost
sacramental--witness the reply of Icilius to Numitorius'
praise of his personal merit:

> You give me (noble Lord) that character
> Which I cood never yet read in my selfe:
> But from your censure shall I take much care
> To adorne it with the fairest ornaments
> Of unambitious vertue: here I hold [He takes Virginia's
>
> hand.]
>
> My honorable patterne, one whose minde
> Appeares more like a ceremonious chappell
> Full of sweet musick, then a thronging presence.
> I am confirm'd, the court doth make some shew
> Fairer then else they would doe; but her port
> Being a simple virtue, beautifies the court.[7]
>
> (I, ii, 7-17)

And Virginia's reply is precisely what we would expect it
to be:

> It is a flattery (my Lord)
> You breath upon me, and it shewes much like
> The borrowed painting which some Ladies use--
> It is not to continue many dayes;
> My wedding garments will outweare this praise.
>
> (I, ii, 18-22)

Their idyllic scene is rudely shattered by the
report that Virginia's father has arrived in great haste
at Rome. The suspense leads into scene iii, where they
learn that Virginius has gone directly to the Senate. His
arrival has excited the mob:

> . . . troopes of artisans
> Follow his panting horse, and with a strang,
> Confused noyse, partly with joy to see him,
> Partly with fear for what his hast portends,
> 'They shew as if a sudden mutiny
> Orespread the City.
>
> (I, ii, 28-33)

Never actually seen on stage, the mob is an ever-present
reality in the play; in nearly every scene it is either
heard or reported, or as in the climactic scenes, both.
Throughout the play, the city plebeians and the mutinous
soldiers are paralleled, constant reminders of the demands
upon the skill and integrity of those in command. (In
Act V, camp and city are finally brought face to face
within the city itself.)

Scenes iii and iv of Act I juxtapose the private
and public Appius; in iii he confides to his evil genius,
Clodius:

> I am at much variance
> Within my selfe, there's discord in my blood,

My powers are all in combat, I have nothing

Left but sedition in me.

(I, iii, 6-9)

Webster does not want an Angelo, however, and Appius' lust

for Virginia, the source of his internal discord, never

becomes more than simply the motive for his plotting, which

is got under way at once. By making Clodius the chief

plotter, Webster protects Appius from becoming a comic

Machiavel. Their first ploy is to use control of the pub-

lic Treasury to force Virginius to make a path for Appius

to his daughter. Virginius makes his plea, and Appius

makes his move by denying the old man on grounds that his

language is intemperate. Virginius answers him in a long

and threatening speech on the consequences of arbitrary

rule. The Senate will not hear him, and he is left alone

on stage to speculate like a Coriolanus on the sad plight

of the soldier:

What slave would be a soldier to be censured

By such as ne'er saw danger! To have our pay,

Our worths and merits ballanc'd in the scale

Of base moth-eaten peace! I have had wounds

Would have made all this Bench faint and look pale

But to behold them searcht. They lay their heads

On their soft pillowes, pore upon their bags,

Grow fat with laziness and resty ease.
          to
And/us that stand betwixt them and disaster

They will not spare a <u>Drachma</u>. O my souldiers,
Before you want, I'l sell my smal possessions
Even to my skin, to help you--Plate and Jewels
All shall be yours. Men that are men indeed,
The earth shal find, the Sun and air must feed.

(I, iv, 108-21)

The conclusion of Act 1 brings together Virginius,
his immediate family, and Icilius in the otherwise deserted
Senate. When Virginia kneels to him for blessing, he addresses her and Icilius in terms which suggest the ideal
marriage of city, court, and military:

Daughter rise.
And, brother, I am only rich in her,
And in your love, link't with the honour'd friendship
Of these fair Romane Lords. For you <u>Icilius</u>,
I hear I must adopt you with the title
Of a new son; you are <u>Virginia's</u> chief,
And I am proud she hath built her fair election
Upon such a store of vertues. May you grow,
Although a Cities child, to know a souldier
And rate him to his merit.

(I, iv, 125-34)

But there is something perfunctory here which suggests
his words are merely a pious hope, spoken for the immediate
occasion. And this is confirmed by the fact that he must

leave at once for the camp, without even waiting on the
wedding feast, to put down the threatening mutiny.

This concluding scene of Act I completes the configuration of the basic conflict of the play. Roman virtue,
nourished for centuries by military threat without and the
dangers of faction within, is depicted here as seriously
weakened, and the sign of the spreading sickness is the
isolation of the normally responsible elements and the
consequent tyranny of Appius and his dependents. Not until
the time of Julius Caesar will the Roman mob have permanent
control of power, making the rule of Augustus almost foreordained, as both Webster and Shakespeare appear to have
understood. In the Rome of this play, the unruly mob and
the mutinous soldiers represent threats of violence rather
than serious contenders for power.

3

The action of the play, then, up until the courtroom
climax in Act IV, consists of a detailed development of the
conflict set up in Act I. Appius plots, and because of his
political skill and the advantage of office, he appears to
be gaining, slowly but surely. Virginia shows herself to
be proof against every inducement. The fullest development
is that of Icilius, however, whose courage and intelligence
and steadfastness are impressive indeed. But in spite of
all, the forces for good are seen to be pathetically

disadvantaged by the antagonists. The close-up glimpses
of life among the servants and in the camp serve to flesh
out the image of disorder attendant upon the confusion of
the established hierarchy when people of estate and reputation are publicly seized and brought before the dock.

The lengthy trial scene which takes up most of
Act IV is the best thing in the play, despite the traditional critical bias in favor of the more naturalistic
arrest of Virginia in the marketplace.[8] The plotters
attempt to prove Virginia to be the base-born child of a
slave rather than the child of Virginius. What emerges
is a demonstration that any story can be made to appear
valid enough for all practical purposes, if the staging
be carefully enough managed. And it is not the fact of
his evil intentions, or a power for good operative in the
nature of the universe, which defeats Appius, but, rather,
the unpredictable element latent in all human affairs,
the cloud no bigger than a man's fist that even the most
watchful attender will sooner or later fail to note.

Virginius, isolated by the seizure of Icilius for
speaking out publicly against Appius, recognizing he is
about to be defeated, publicly slaughters his daughter
to save her from dishonor.

In the confusion, Virginius escapes the city and
appears before his disorganized troops, begging that he
be put out of his misery. The camp, against him at first,
soon swears its loyalty and urges him to lead them against

the city for revenge. Act IV closes with Virginius'
acceptance--

> I accept your choice, in hope to guard you all
> From my inhumane sufferings. Be't my pride
> That I have bred a daughter whose chast blood
> Was spilt for you, and for Romes lasting good.
>
> (IV, ii, 204-07)

However personally satisfactory such a solution, it is
one which bodes ill for justice and the commonweal. The
politically meaningful possibilities are presented in the
dialectic of Act V, which is what makes it rather than
Acts III or IV, however dramatic, the true focus of interest of the play.

Act V consists of only two scenes, each of which
is less than 200 lines. Scene i takes place in the Forum;
Scene ii in the prison where Appius and Clodius, who have
been seized and imprisoned by the men of the city led by
Icilius and Numitorius, await their fates. A series of
confrontations take place, building throughout the act
toward the final disposition of the guilty and the re-
integration of society at the close of the play.

The first confrontation, which is something of
a preliminary, takes place between the Advocate who served
the corrupted Appius in his attempt against Virginia and
two Senators. The Advocate boasts that since he knows

how to shape himself to the needs of the time, he need
fear no change in the political climate. He plans, moreover, to deliver an oration in the market-place, before
the newly arrived troops, and so make his fortune with the
new rulers. We have seen before, in The White Devil and
in the Act IV trial scene of this play, something of what
Webster seems to have felt about the power of rhetoric
and the uses of that power. But here there is a new and
different tone. The Advocate is depicted here as a fool;
his, would seem to be the ultimate foolishness of buying
his own bill of goods. Thus Webster appears to dismiss
the paid Advocate and his counterfeit rhetoric in a tone
of comic raillery--witness the final words directed to
him as he disappears from the play:

> Farewel Proteus,
> And I shall wish thy eloquent bravado
> May sheild thee from the whip and Bastinado.
> Now in this furious tempest let us glide,
> With foulded sails at pleasure of the Tyde.
>
> (V, i, 57-61)

Those who know better, such as the speaker of the
above, prepare to weather the tempest as best they can.
The point is well taken: in crises of public upheaval,
only the fool believes that anything is foreordained, or
that a man may reasonably expect to control his own fate.

Now, in the second and major confrontation of Scene
i, the two main factions--the city, led by Icilius and
Numitorius, and the military, led by Virginius--enter from
opposite sides. A parley is called and the concluding
action begins.

Earlier, in the speeches of the corrupt public
officials, in language which echoes the mad Lear, Webster
defined the peculiar madness of the tyrant: one who identi-
fies with the public office 'so completely that he cannot
make the distinction between his own concerns and the concerns of the office. The inevitable consequence is the
wish to see the whole social and political structure
destroyed if the tyrant fail to realize his ends.

CLOD. Were there no more men to support great Rome,
Even failling Rome should perish, ere he stand:
I'l after him, and kill him.

(II, iii, 189-91)

APP. . . .
Should I miscarry in this desperate plot,
This of my fate in after times be spoken,
I'l break that with my weight on which I am broken.

(III, iii, 30-32)

The labyrinth of Act V is to complicate infinitely the
question of power, however, by revealing that even the
most selfless, just, and righteous of men is capable of

a similar distortion of values. The question of revenge
is of central importance here. Both Icilius and Virginius
feel personally entitled to revenge, and each is backed
by a powerful faction. Virginius is heard first; like
Lear, he is feverish in mind and body.

> NUMIT. How is it with your sorrow noble brother?
> VIRG. I am forsaken of the gods, old man.
> NUMIT. Preach not that wretched doctrine to your selfe.
> It will beget despaire.
> VIRG. What doe you call
> A burning Feaver? Is not that a divel?
> It shakes me like an Earthquake. Wilt a, wilt a?
> Give me some Wine.
> NUMIT. O it is hurtful for you!
> VIRG. Why so are all things that the appetite
> Of man doth covet in his perfect'st health
> Whatever Nature or Art have invented,
> To make the boundless wish of man contented,
> Are all his poison. Give me the Wine there.--When!
> Do you grudge me a poor cup of drink? Say, say.
> Now by the gods, I'll leave enough behind me
> To pay my debts, and for the rest, no matter
> Who scrambles for't.[9]
> NUMIT. Here my noble brother!
> Alas, your hand shakes. I will guide it to you.
> VIRG. 'Tis true, it trembles. Welcome thou just palsies

'Twere pity this should doe me longer service,

Now it hath slain my daughter. So, I thank you;

Now I have lost all comforts in the world,

It seems I must a little longer live,

Bee't but to serve my belly.

(V, i, 72-97)

Virginius has taken the lead, but he shows himself to be
emotionally and physically near to exhaustion. He is
clearly confused about the issues at stake and cannot
reconcile his divided loyalties. He speaks cynically.
His hand must be steadied to keep him from spilling the
wine, and it is clear that he is in need of an understanding greater than his own to guide his leadership. He is
only vaguely aware of the dilemma he faces: to secure
his honor he must have revenge. But honor requires a context, a city, to assure that it will survive the lifetime
of the individual. And if Rome is to be immortal, her
laws must be secure. How may the imperatives of personal
honor and public safety both be satisfied?

When Icilius speaks it is to tax Virginius with
the "unnatural and damnable" murder of his daughter.
Virginius replies by reasserting his original position,
that since he acted in the name of justice and nobility,
"posterity which truely renders/ To each man his desert,
shal praise me for't." Icilius persists, and Virginius
charges him with defaulting on his oath of knighthood:

. . . You are a <u>Roman</u> Knight.

What was your oath when you receiv'd your Knighthood?

A parcel of it is, as I remember,

Rather to die with honour, then to live

In servitude. Had my poor girle been ravish'd,

In her dishonour, and in my sad griefe,

Your love and pity quickly had ta'ne end.

Great mens misfortunes thus have ever stood,

They touch none neerly, but their neerest blood.

, What do you meane to do? It seems, my Lord,

Now you have caught the sword within your hand,

Like a madman you'le draw it to offend

Those that best love you; and perhaps the counsel

Of some loose unthrifts, and vile malecontents

Heartens you to't: goe to, take your course,

My faction shal not give the least advantage

To murtherers, to banqueroots, or thieves,

To fleece the Common-Wealth.

(V, i, 125-43)

Thus he states the case for traditional rights: Since
the patrician has always ventured the most, he has the
greatest claim to rule. He concludes with the traditional
defense--that <u>any</u> change must lead inevitably to anarchy.

The stalemate appears complete as Icilius pleads
that Virginius' use of force to impose his right is the
real danger to the body politic. Against Virginius'

absolute claim, for himself and the patrician class, Icilius
urges the rights of the city and impersonal law:

> O you gods!
>
> You are now a General; learn to know your place,
>
> And use your noble calling modestly.
>
> Better had Appius been an upright Judg,
>
> And yet an evil man, then honest man,
>
> And yet a dissolute Judg; for all disgrace
>
> Lights losse upon the person, then the place.
>
> You are i' th' City now, where if you raise
>
> But the least uproare, even your Fathers house
>
> Shal not be free from ransack. Piteous fires
>
> That chance in Towrs of stone, are not so feared
>
> As those that light in Flax-shaps; for there's food
>
> for eminent ruin.
>
> (V, i, 154-66)

The final image is interesting for the way it renders a
city reality in metaphoric terms,[10] extending out to include
the rulers themselves within the implications of the figure.

The immediate conflict is resolved by Icilius, who
declares his love for Virginius but continues to refuse
to shake his bloodied hand. His concluding speech here
is especially noteworthy for the insight it offers on the
opposing claims of personal grief and public duty. To
dwell obsessively on private sorrow is to forget the just
demands of the public world. (Shakespeare's Richard of

Bordeaux comes immediately to mind.)

> To th' Senate. Come, no more of this sad tale,
> For such a tel-tale may we term our grief,
> And doth as 'twere so listen to her own words,
> Envious of others sleep, because shee wakes.
> I ever would converse with a griev'd person
> In a longe journey to beguile the day,
> Or winter evening to passe time away.
> March on, and let proud <u>Appius</u> in our view
> Like a tree rotted, fall that way he grew.
>
> (V, i, 183-91)

The function of the final couplet is to link up the
abstract questions involved with the immediate issue, the
judgment and execution of Appius.

4

The opening forty lines of the final scene of the
play contain a dialogue between Appius and Clodius on the
uncertainties of fortune. They are at first agreed that
the fault lay with the "Hydra-headed multitude," the
"inconsistent rabble." But they end by turning upon one
another. At this point Icilius and Virginius enter with
their respective factions. Their first concern is the
control of the mob which, incapable of reason and justice,

> Would ruine this stone building and drag hence
> This impious Judg, piece-meal to tear his limbs
> Before the Law convince him.
>
> (V, ii, 44-46)

Allowed to speak in his own behalf, Appius con-
fesses his guilt and pleads to Virginius for mercy on the
grounds that every man in high place is particularly exposed to the vagaries of fortune. Virginius answers in
terms which recall his previous expressions of moral relativism, wherein he was wont to ascribe all to chance:

> Uncertain fate!--but yesterday his breath
> Aw'd Rome, and his least torved frown was death:
> I cannot chuse but pity and lament,
> So high a rise should have such low discent.
>
> (V, ii, 66-69)

Icilius' reaction correctly locates the source of Virginius'
pity in the sentimentality which is the other side of an
uncontrolled desire for revenge. Both may be commendable
as private virtues, but both are dangerous indeed when
carried into the public realm. Like the plotters in
Shakespeare's Julius Caesar, Virginius confuses the issues.
The transition Webster is objectifying here entails the
reinstatement of the old values on a new power base, one
which clearly is neither modern nor ancient. Webster's
new "egalitarian" ideal is aware of the pressure of the

commons, but disdains to make use of them in the manner
of Julius Caesar. Such a solution, as Shakespeare appears
to have understood, made traditional patrician virtue
superfluous. But the Rome of Caesar and Augustus is still
centuries in the future for Webster's historic setting.

Numitorius is unable to resolve the problem, but
he does manage to state the issue rather explicitly:

> Virginius, you are too remiss to punish
> Deeds of this nature. You must fashion now
> 'Your actions to your place, not to your passion--
> Severity to such acts is as necessary
> As pity to the tears of innocence.
>
> (V, ii, 80-84)

Meanwhile, Icilius has gone to bring the body of
Virginia to witness against Appius and recover Virginius
to his duty. As he approaches through the clogged streets,
the sound of the mob's lamenting is borne in upon the
assemblage, emphasizing both the immediate danger and something more important--the possibility of a rebirth of an
authority secured and sanctified by the innocent blood of
the slain Virginia.[11] The group on stage is as yet only
aware of the first, however, the immediate danger, and
soldiers are dispatched to keep order in the streets.

The sight of the body causes Virginius to fall
into a passion once again, but Icilius brings him up short
with the imperative,

> Leave this passion,
>
> Proceed to your sentence.
>
> (V, ii, 113-14)

The condmened are offered swords with which to execute
each other. Appius is redeemed in death by his killing
himself. The base-born Clodius turns coward, fearing to
die because of what may come after death. The message is
clear--to practice virtue out of fear of punishment and
expectation of reward after death is base motive indeed.
His final argument is familiar enough to us:

> For mercy, mercy I intreat you all.
>
> Is't not sufficient for Virginia slain
>
> That Appius suffered; one of noble blood,
>
> And eminence in place, for a Plebeian?
>
> Besides, he was my Lord and might command me:
>
> If I did ought, 'twas by compulsion, Lords,
>
> And therefore I crave mercy.
>
> (V, ii, 158-64)

When Icilius speaks his doom, his own "nobility" is obvious
in his words; and so is Webster's personal conviction
about breeding:

> Then I sentence thus:
>
> Thou hadst a mercy, most unmerriting slave,
>
> Of which thy base birth was not capable,

Which we take off by taking thence thy sword.

And note the difference 'twixt a noble strain,

And one bred from the rabble: both alike

Dar'd to transgresse, but see their odds in death:

Appius dy'd like a Roman Gentleman,

And a man both wayes knowing; but this slave

Is only sensible of vitious living,

Not apprehensive of a noble death.

Therefore as a base Malefactor we

, And timorous slave, give him (as he deserves)

Unto the common hangman.

(V, ii, 164-80)

Clodius is dragged away and the concluding passages signal the simultaneous death of the old order and rebirth of the new.

ICIL. Away with him: the life of the Decemviri

Expires in them. Rome thou at length art free.

Restored unto thine ancient liberty. . . .

MINUT. Of consuls: which bold Junius Brutus first

Begun in Tarquins fall. Virginius you

And young Icilius shall his place succeed,

So by the peoples suffrage 'tis decreed.

VIRG. We martial then our souldiers in that name

Of Consuls, honoured with those golden bayes.

Two Ladies fair, but most infortunate,

Have in their ruins rais'd declining <u>Rome</u>--

<u>Lucretia</u> and <u>Virginia</u>, both renown'd

For chastity. Souldiers and noble Romans,

To grace her death, whose life hath freed great <u>Rome</u>,

March with her Corse to her sad Funeral Tomb.

(V, ii, 183-97)

The linking of Lucretia and Virginia here suggests some of the symbolic significance of chastity, an almost obsessive idea in Webster's tragedy. First of all the implications for the lady herself: a sign of self-denial, chastity is particularly meaningful in the great because they are more severely tempted. Chastity can also be a sign of nobility in the low-born; without the example of the great, however, such virtue in society is hardly to be expected.[12] Chastity also symbolizes in Webster the uncontaminated source, the crucial importance of which is that it makes the possibility of rebirth an ever-present potential. It is here that private and public virtues intersect, usually finding outward expression in concern for name and reputation.

In the earlier tragedies, where he was at once more passionate and more uncertain, Webster combined both active and passive virtues in his central female figure. Here he has relegated his feminine protagonist almost wholly to the position of passive victim. Because of her murder, father and aggrieved husband must oppose each other. The

question of whether Icilius shall have revenge at the price
of civil disorder is raised by locating the opposition
in a conflict between her father and her husband, who represent the patrician and merchant classes respectively.
When the old man wavers in executing justice on the tyrant
Appius, it is the sight of the murdered Virginia's body,
carried through the public streets in full view of all by
Icilius, which steadies Virginius' resolve and, finally,
sanctifies the new political order.

5

The implications for my thesis must be more than
clear by now: the dialectic of Appius and Virginia, the
last of Webster's three tragedies, both clarifies his con-
ceptual frame of reference and resolves the tragic conflict
of the earlier period. Although the comparison is doubtless extreme, the final play of the Oresteia comes to mind.
In Webster, too, violence has yielded to persuasion and
private vengeance given way to public justice. Despite
the classical setting and legendary Roman characters and
plot, the contingencies are Webster's own in Appius and
Virginia, just as they are in the earlier two plays.

Nothing so easy as a marriage of convenience between an heir of the older nobility and a gentleman of the
city, however, would serve to express Webster's resolution.
The new egalitarian mythos required reason,[13] in addition

to the authority of class distinction, and the sanctity
of blood sacrifice. But some kind of public test and
certification is required, hence the function of Webster's
trial scenes. The confusion of appearance and reality
characteristic of the Machiavellian worlds of The White
Devil and The Duchess of Malfi made such certitude impossible, with the attendant dislocations and confusion of
values we have seen in connection with those earlier poetic
visions of the world. The realization of disinterested
justice and exemplary rule implied im the image of political
rebirth in Appius and Virginia may, however, indicate nothing
personally more significant for the poet than an appeal to the
popular market, a celebration of popular pieties.

It seems to me, however, that this particular image
of the good society is more significant than this, especially
when viewed against the important early tragedies. In the
early two tragedies, Webster is looking at the corruption of
the court, a corruption which he feels must permeate all of
society; worse still, he can find no way out. A corrupt
court makes impossible any redemptive process, since each new
potential ruler must himself be corrupted by the atmosphere
at court. Whatever shift of power occurs accomplishes
little, therefore. But with the passing of a generation,
a new political vision suggests itself. (Perhaps it would
be more accurate to say that, with the passing of a political
generation, Webster was enabled to see the possibility which

was in a process of becoming all along.) A new group comes
into power and the political realignment which accompanies
this transition brings into being a new set of "reigning
fictions" to lend it legitimacy. For the playwright, the
new vision offers new hope, hence the relaxation of tragic
inevitability. The final play is a celebration of the new
order, of the way things are to be, and this involves the
celebration of community rather than tragic inevitability.

The crisis of authority felt by Webster and many of
his contemporaries with the demise of the divine right myth
in England passed, and with it, if we can judge by this last
tragedy, Webster's sense of tragic uncertainty.[14] To the
more or less permanent gulf which came into being between
the ruler and the office[15] after Machiavelli's thought made
the ancient identification of the two no longer possible,
we may trace the end of a tragic perspective available to
both Classical and Renaissance poets. Thus it is that
Madeleine Doran's definition of the nexus of tragedy as

. . . the lust for power, the corrupting effects of
power, both on the holders of power and on their followers, the conflict between the drive and insight
of a great man and the limitations of authority and
of man-made laws,[16]

however useful for the Elizabethan-Jacobean kind, is recognizably inadequate to describe tragedy since then.[17]

Webster's great tragedies were possible because the split in consciousness which began with Machiavelli had not as yet become permanent, making it inevitable that a radical examination of political man should lead directly to an examination of the whole human condition.

NOTES TO CHAPTER IV

[1]*Works*, III, 121-30. John Russell Brown, editor
of the most recent edition of Webster's The White Devil
(Cambridge, 1960), supports Lucas in this dating: "It
might have been written as early as 1603-4, but the weight
of evidence is in favour of a date many years after The
White Devil, in the late twenties or early thirties" ("Introduction," pp. xviii-xix).

[2]Despite William Archer's perverse judgment that
this is the best of Webster's plays, I find myself in
essential agreement with Lucas on the question of its merit:

> "But Appius remains a very worthy piece, the work of a
> quite competent talent with no flicker of genius left,
> a very adequate handling of a not very brilliant theme.
> . . . The third and last of Webster's tragedies remains,
> then, the least faulty, but certainly not the best of
> his works" (Works, III, 146-47).

[3]"Fundamental Interpretations of the Tragic," from
Tragedy is Not Enough, reprinted in The Art of the Theater,
ed. by R. W. Corrigan and J. L. Rosenberg (San Francisco,
1964), p. 471.

[4]No one would deny the poetic power of Sophocles'
Antigone, for instance, where the center is clearly not
character as such. Roy Morrell states it concisely:
"Character, or some figure or idea [my italics] in which

the audience can identify themselves exactly as in a great
character, is indispensable to tragedy; it must not dominate the action, but it is, despite Aristotle, as indispensable as action" ("The Psychology of Tragic Pleasure,"
reprinted in Tragedy: Modern Essays in Criticism, ed. L.
Michel and R. B. Sewall, Englewood Cliffs, 1963, p. 289).

For a good comprehensive summary of the relevant
criticism on the problem of tragic form generally and the
questions of genre, the tragic hero, and the possibility
of a specifically political tragedy in particular, see
Sewall, pp. 344-48.

[5]Works, III, 225; see also pp. 131-33 for Lucas'
full treatment of Webster's source, a question he appears
to have settled definitively.

[6]Works, III, 132.

[7]Lucas discusses the anachronism in the reference
to the court here in connection with the date of composition; his point has to do with the problem of borrowings
(Works, III, 128). What seems striking to me, however, is
the relative scarcity of such references in this play.
Several possibilities suggest themselves, although rather
too easily for comfort: (a) the increased loss of power
and prestige of the court by this late date; (b) Webster's
growing indifference, for whatever personal reasons;
(c) the possibility that Webster was comfortable enough with
the new "reigning fictions," a possibility supported by

the play itself I believe, to enable him to get out from
under, so to speak, his almost compulsive fascination with
the court.

[8]The older critics appear to have fixed on the
arrest scene with the same unanimity of appreciation (see
Works, III, p. 147) they have shown for the Act III quarrel
scene of the lovers in The White Devil. The bias in
both cases seems to me primarily a consequence of character-
oriented readings. For the earlier play, such a bias does
little harm; probably it is a much less damaging bias than
my own. For this play, however, this Romantic focus is
indeed confusing. My personal preference for the trial
scene and, I might add, the entire final act, must be obvious from my reading of the play. In my own defense,
though, I would add only that I feel the trial scene is
dramatically compelling precisely because of its artificiality.

[9]Virginius' speech here is the closest the play
approaches the more or less typical Elizabethan-Jacobean
tragedy of personal conflict. Compare Fulke Greville's,

"Oh, wearisome conditions of humanity!

Born under one law, to another bound

Vainly begot and yet forbidden vanity:

Created sick, commanded to be sound.

What meaneth Nature by these diverse laws--

Passion and reason, self-division's clause?"

As I have indicated, the self-division of Appius is handled
so matter-of-factly as to be almost academic. Icilius remains the melodramatic good man throughout, a good choice
for a post on the Chamber of Commerce. And as Lucas describes it, Virginia is "killed almost before she knows
her fate," and therefore is "unable to suffer even the in-
ward struggles of an Iphigenia, whose first maiden terror
we can watch rising into heroism" (Works, III, 147). Finally,
Virginius' farewell to his daughter (IV, i, 321-36) is consistent with his character, being more pathetic than tragic.
It is, however, a lovely passage and perfectly consistent
with Webster's general purpose in the play.

Appius logically should provide the tragic focus
but, unhappily, does not. His effective early speeches are
directed to the condition of the statesman generally,
rather than to any particular conflict. And the division
he feels within himself is never linked up with any conflict we might expect from his misuse of power. His death
speech touches on all the appropriate issues, but in a
perfunctory, academic fashion.

[10] Indeed, Lucas (Works, III, 126) finds in this
image a possible allusion to a specific warehouse confla-
gration impressive and costly enough to be mentioned prom-
inently in several extant accounts. For my reading of
the play, however, the image is meaningful for the way in
which it summarizes the opposition between the patrician-

soldier, who must be reminded of what a city is in human terms, and the gentleman-citizen, who is only too aware of the cost.

[11]Were it not for the democratic anachronism, Melville's Billy Budd would offer a precise analogue. If we put aside the composition of the particular social classes involved in the two works, the analogue is useful, I think. Melville like Webster is interested in the process of political myth formation: his long digression on the death of Nelson and his contrasting of the official and the private accounts of Billy's death do more than merely suggest this. Moreover, Melville also seems aware of the difficulty of bridging the gulf between the public and the private.

[12]This serves to clarify the symbolism of Virginius and Virginia's appearing at court costumed as slaves, which, despite the Roman historical precedent, is obviously meaningful beyond mere atmosphere. It is suggestive also in respect to the particulars of the charges brought against the dead mother of Virginia which, though Webster did not invent, he certainly did choose to emphasize.

[13]If we are reminded here of Hobbes, and the structure and ideals of the Leviathan (reason, equity, justice, civil peace, the requirements of the market, and a bourgeois model of man and society), we should not be too surprised, for, according to C. B. Macpherson, "there is considerable evidence

that Hobbes' central political doctrine had been received
and ingested, much more fully than is generally recognized,
into the main stream of serious political thinking in his
own lifetime." Hobbes Leviathan (Penguin Books, 1968), Introduction, p. 24.

[14]In defense of my own speculations, then, I offer
the following brief passage from Hannah Arendt: ". . . to
live in a political realm with neither authority nor the
concomitant awareness that the source of authority transcends power and those who are in power, means to be con-
fronted anew, without the religious trust in a sacred
beginning and without the protection of traditional and
therefore self-evident standards of behavior, by the ele-
mentary problems of human living-together" (Between Past
and Future, p. 141).

[15]Webster makes this insight quite explicit, it
seems to me, in a speech uttered by Icilius at a critical
juncture in the play:

"Better had Appius been an upright Judg,

And yet an evil man, then honest man,

And yet a dissolute Judg. . . ."

(V, i, 157-59)

Perhaps I overestimate--Icilius does, however,
appear to be the chief spokesman for the values of reason
and order in the play.

[16]Endeavors of Art, p. 124.

[17]Reviewing Auerbach and Fergusson on the whole question of the link between culture and representation in literature, Levi writes:

> "The phrase 'partial perspectives' is important, for it indicates a fact which Fergusson and Auerbach both know; the fragmentation of modern culture. And it suggests that the weakness of our general intellectual life may mean not so much literal weakness as diversification--the lack of a central tendency or dominant
> , moral concern, and a plurality of philosophical perspectives which conditions our approach to literary and artistic experience because it conditions contemporary life . . ." (pp. 260-61).

Webster's is a "partial perspective" in Appius and Virginia, but as I have been arguing, it may well have been the process of fragmentation itself which triggered his creative impulse ten or fifteen years earlier.

BIBLIOGRAPHY

Works by Webster

The Complete Works of John Webster. Edited by F. L. Lucas.
4 Vols. London, 1928.

Other Works Cited

Abel, Lionel. Metatheater. New York, 1964.

Abrams, M. H. The Mirror and the Lamp. New York, 1953.

Arendt, Hannah. Between Past and Future: Six Exercises
in Political Thought. Cleveland & New York, 1963.

_____. The Human Condition. Garden City, 1958.

Bogard, Travis. The Tragic Satire of John Webster.
Berkeley, 1955.

Boklund, Gunnar. The Sources of The White Devil. Uppsala,
1957.

Brown, J. R. and Harris, B. (eds.). Jacobean Theatre.
London, 1960.

Brown, John Russell (ed.). The White Devil. London, 1960.

Butterfield, Herbert. The Statecraft of Machiavelli.
New York, 1962.

Campbell, Joseph. The Hero With a Thousand Faces. Cleveland and New York, 1956.

Cassirer, Ernst. The Individual and the Cosmos in Renaissance Philosophy. Trans. Mario Domandi. New York,
1963.

_____. The Myth of the State. Garden City, 1955.

_____. The Philosophy of Symbolic Forms. 3 Vols.
Trans. Ralph Manheim. New Haven, 1953-57.

Chabod, Federico. Machiavelli and the Renaissance. Trans.
David Moore. London, 1958.

Cook, Albert. The Dark Voyage and the Golden Mean: A Philosophy of Comedy. Cambridge, 1949.

Corrigan, R. W. and Rosenberg, J. L. (eds.) The Art of the Theater. San Francisco, 1964.

Cruttwell, Patrick. The Shakespearean Moment. New York, 1960.

Cunliffe, John W. The Influence of Seneca on Elizabethan Tragedy. New York, 1893.

Davis, Godfrey. The Early Stuarts: 1603-1660. Oxford, 1937.

Dean, Leonard F. Elizabethan Drama. New York, 1950.

_____. (ed. and trans.). The Praise of Folly by Desiderius Erasmus. New York, 1946.

_____. "Richard II: The State and the Image of the Theater," PMLA, Vol. 67, 1952.

de Jouvenel, Bertrand. On Power: Its Nature and the History of its Growth. Trans. J. F. Huntington. Boston, 1962.

_____. The Pure Theory of Politics. New Haven, 1963.

Dent, R. W. John Webster's Borrowings. Berkeley, 1960.

Doran, Madeleine. Endeavors of Art: A Study of Form in Elizabethan Drama. Madison, 1954.

Ellis-Fermor, Una. The Frontiers of Drama. New York, 1946.

_____. The Jacobean Drama. London, 1936.

Farnham, Willard. The Medieval Heritage of Elizabethan Tragedy. Berkeley, 1936.

Fergusson, Francis. The Human Image in Dramatic Literature. Garden City, 1957.

_____. The Idea of a Theater. Princeton, 1949.

Figgis, J. N. The Divine Right of Kings. Cambridge, 1896.

_____. Studies of Political Thought from Gerson to Grotius: 1414-1625. New York, 1960.

Frye, Northrup. Anatomy of Criticism. Princeton, 1957.

_____. The Critical Path. Bloomington and London, 1971.

_____. The Educated Imagination. Toronto, 1963.

_____. Fables of Identity. New York, 1963.

Goddard, Harold C. The Meaning of Shakespeare. Vol. II. Chicago and London, 1951.

Gombrich, E. H. Meditations on a Hobby Horse, and Other Essays on the Theory of Art. London, 1963.

Ortega y Gassett, Jose. Man and Crisis. Trans. Mildred Adams. New York, 1958.

_____. Meditations on Quixote. New York, 1961.

_____. The Modern Theme. Trans. James Cleugh. New York, 1933.

Hall, Vernon. Renaissance Literary Criticism. Gloucester, Mass., 1959.

Harris, Victor. All Coherence Gone. Chicago, 1949.

Haydn, Hiram. The Counter-Renaissance. New York, 1960

Hebel, J. W., and Hudson, H. H. (ed.). Poetry of the English Renaissance. New York, 1929.

Huxley, Aldous. Collected Essays. New York, 1958.

James, D. G. The Dream of Learning. Oxford, 1951.

Kaufmann, R. J. "The Seneca Perspective and the Shakespearean Poetic," Comparative Drama, I, No. 3.

_____. "Tragedy and Its Validating Conditions," Comparative Drama, I, No. 1.

Knights, L. C. Drama and Society in the Age of Jonson. London, 1937.

Koyre, Alexander. The Closed World to the Infinite Universe. Baltimore, 1957.

Langer, Susanne K. Feeling and Form. New York, 1955.

Lawlor, John. The Tragic Sense in Shakespeare. New York, 1960.

Leech, Clifford. John Webster: A Critical Study. London, 1951.

Levi, Albert Wm. Literature, Philosophy and the Imagination. Bloomington, 1962.

Lewis, C. S. The Discarded Image. Cambridge, 1964.

Lovejoy, A. O. The Great Chain of Being. Cambridge, 1936.

Macklen, Michael. The Anatomy of the World. Minneapolis, 1958.

Macpherson, C. B. Hobbes Leviathan. Baltimore, 1968.

Meisel, James. The Myth of the Ruling Class: Gaetano Mosca and the Elite. Ann Arbor, 1958.

Michel, L., and Sewall, R. B. (eds.). Tragedy: Modern Essays in Criticism. Englewood Cliffs, 1963.

Murry, H. A. Myth and Mythmaking. New York, 1960.

Olschki, Leonardo. Machiavelli the Scientist. Berkeley, 1945.

Olson, Elder. Tragedy and the Theory of Drama. Detroit, 1961.

Ornstein, Robert. The Moral Vision of Jacobean Tragedy. Madison, 1960.

Palmer, John. Political and Comic Characters of Shakespeare. London, 1962.

Raab, Felix. The English Face of Machiavelli, A Changing Interpretation, 1500-1700. London, 1964.

Ribner, Irving R. Jacobean Tragedy: The Quest for Moral Order. London, 1962.

Rosenberg, Harold. The Tradition of the New. New York, 1959.

Rosen, William. Shakespeare and the Craft of Tragedy. Cambridge, 1960.

Rossiter, A. P. Angel with Horns and Other Shakespeare Lectures. Ed. Graham Storey. New York, 1961.

Sewall, Richard. "The Tragic Form," Essays in Criticism, IV, No. 4.

Sewell, Arthur. Character and Society in Shakespeare. London, 1951.

Siegel, Paul N. Shakespearean Tragedy and the Elizabethan Compromise. New York, 1957.

Spencer, Theodore. Shakespeare and the Nature of Man. New York, 1942.

Stone, Lawrence. The Crisis of the Aristocracy: 1558-1641. Oxford, 1965.

_____. "History a la Mode," The New York Review of Books, Vol. III, No. 2.

Strauss, Leo. Thoughts on Machiavelli. Glencoe, Ill., 1958.

Styan, J. L. The Elements of Drama. Cambridge, 1960.

Thorndike, Ashley H. Tragedy. Boston, 1908.

Tillyard, E. M. W. Myth and the English Mind. New York, 1962.

_____. The Elizabethan World Picture. London, 1943.

_____. Shakespeare's History Plays. Baltimore, 1962.

Trilling, Lionel. The Liberal Imagination. New York, 1950.

Weldon, Antony. Secret History of the Court of King James I. 2 Vols. Ed. Sir Walter Scott (?). London, 1811.